Heidelberg

on the Neckar

Illustrated Guide
to Castle and Town

Heidelberg – Schloßaltan

nachTh.Verhas

Edm. von König-Verlag, Heidelberg/Dielheim

A selection of many things worth knowing

Dear Guest,

The ruins of the Heidelberg castle rank with the Acropolis and the palace of Versailles as the sights most worth seeing anywhere in Europe. The number of visitors is estimated at more than 3 million every year. They stand in the centre of a breath-taking composition of river and hill, a jumble of roofs and the tranquil greenery of the forest. Numerous poets such as Scheffel, von Brentano, Arnim, Görres, Hölderlin, Eichendorff, and Jean Paul have sung the praises of the city and the castle ruins, and have turned Heidelberg into the quintessence of the German Romantic period.

The University has also contributed a great deal to the world-wide recognition enjoyed by the city all over the world. It was founded in 1386, making it Germany's oldest university.

Heidelberg regards the reputation it holds as an obligation, and this applies particularly to the sphere of the cultural facilities it offers. In addition to outstanding productions by the Städtische Bühne (municipal theatre), open air performances in the castle courtyard have earned themselves particular respect. A rich selection greets the music-lover perusing the calendar of events: concerts in the castle, performances by the city orchestra, choirs and musical societies compete with the famous organ concerts in the Heiliggeistkirche. Amongst innumerable exhibitions, two that stand out are the Kurpfälzisches Museum and the University Library, possessing more than 2.2 million books and manuscripts. Lighter entertainment is provided by about a dozen cinemas. Visitors to Heidelberg are informed about the events on offer and the availability of advance ticket sales by an up-to-date calendar of events.

For conferences, the city has a congress centre at its disposal with ultra-modern equipment. Recreational facilities such as 4 indoor swimming-pools, 2 open-air pools, 600 kilometres of paths for walking complete with car-parks, poster-sized maps, exercise tracks, and barbecue corners offer guests not only plenty of sports centres but also a broad spectrum of attractive leisure facilities. Anyone who prefers to take his time over things should visit the remarkable zoo, boasting its own piece of Africa, a primates house and pools for seals, or the neighbouring botanical garden.

However, the high-point of any visit to Heidelberg has to be a tour of the castle ruins, the Grosser Fass ("big barrel"), and the castle gardens. This can be carried out without a guide, just with this slender book, in about an hour and a half. The tour through the city (from Page 00 onwards) follows the route suggested and signposted by the Heidelberg tourist office. Starting at Universtitätsplatz, it will take about 2 hours excluding any time spent inside buildings. At weekends, visitors to Heidelberg also have the possibility of a guide through the city. Anyone who is not quite so nimble-legged may site back and be chauffeured to the various sites in a bus. In addition to this, the tourist office also arranges occasional tours through parts of the town selected with regard to specific subjects, either on foot or on bicycles.

The town was spared damage during the second world war, but still ha

The world-famous ruins of Heidelberg Castle above the Old Town. In the foreground is the Old Bridge with its historic gateway.

to grapple with traffic problems like any other city. Despite parking space for almost 5000 cars in the various multi-storey and underground carparks in the general area of the Old Town, this capacity is still not sufficient, and visitors by car are offered parking spaces in the outskirts and transport by tram (Park and Ride). Within the city limits as well, visitors should accept the environmentally sensible offer of local public transport, as indeed they should for excursions to the surrounding area.

This booklet is intended to arouse your interest in getting to know the city and its sights in more detail than is possible with a one-day sightseeing trip. We want you, in the words of an old German song, to "lose your heart in Heidelberg." We wish you a very pleasurable stay here, and hope that this brochure will help you along the way.

Historical dates

500,000 BC	In 1907, the lower jaw-bone of homo heidelbergensis was found in a wall near Heidelberg, the earliest evidence of human life ever found in Europe.
5th cent. BC	Celts build a fortress of refuge and place of worship on the Heiligenberg.
circa 80 AD	The Romans maintain a caster (permanent camp) and a signalling tower on the right bank of the Neckar, and build a wooden bridge across the Neckar. The first civilian settlements develop under the protection of the camp. The Romans remain until 260 AD.
5th cent. AD	Beginnings of a permanent settlement.
769	The village of "Bergheim" is mentioned in documents for the first time.
1155	The oldest castle and settlement leave the possession of the Bishops of Worms and are taken over by the house of Hohenstaufen. Konrad, of this dynasty, becomes "Pfalzgraf (Count Palatinate) on the Rhine".
1195	The Palatinate joins the house of Welfen through marriage.
1196	"Heidelberch" is mentioned in a document for the first time. A wooden bridge spans the Neckar.
1214	The county of the Palatinate is taken into the Wittelsbach family under Duke Ludwig I of Bavaria.
1225	A caste above Heidelberg is mentioned in documents.
1255	Division of the lands: Rudolf I (of the main line of succession) becomes Count Palatinate (the Palatinate line).
1303	A document names two castles: one located at the present-day "Molkenkur", the other below it, where the present-day castle ruins stand.
1329	After the Palatinate has been partly under the administration of Emperor Ludwig IV, "the Bavarian", it is finally separated from Bavaria under the "House Treaty of Pavia". The honour of participating in the election of the emperor is to alternate between the two dynasties. Rudolf II ("the Blind") becomes the first Prince Elector of the Palatinate, and rules jointly with Ruprecht I until 1353.
1359	The "Golden Bull", an Imperial Law, grants the two Counts Palatinate extensive rights in "indivisible possession": the rank of Prince Elector, and the offices of arch-marshal, the highest Court in the empire, and of imperial administrator.
14th cent.	A settlement independent of the town forms below the castle and exists until 1743.

6

1386	Founding of the oldest university in present-day Germany by Prince Elector Ruprecht I. It is the third university, after Prague and Vienna, to be founded in the whole German-speaking part of central Europe.
1392	The inhabitants of the village of Bergheim are transferred into the Heidelberg Neustadt ("new town"), thus extending the area of the town from the Grabengasse to the present-day Bismarckplatz.
1400	Prince Elector Ruprecht III becomes King of Germany under the name of Ruprecht I of the Palatinate. Building work starts on the Heiliggeistkirche (Church of the Holy Ghost). After Ruprecht's death in 1410, the Palatinate is divided between his four sons.
1462	Battle of Seckenheim: the armies of the Count Marcher of Baden and the Count of Württemberg are defeated by the Palatinate forces under Prince Elector Friedrich I ("the Victorious").
1508-44	Renovation of the defensive walls and workshop buildings in the castle by Prince Elector Ludwig V.
1518	Luther teaches his theory of justification in Heidelberg, in those days a centre of humanism.
1537	Lightning destroys the higher castle.
1556-59	Prince Elector Otto Heinrich introduces the Reformation and builds arguably the finest Renaissance palace north of the Alps.

Ottheinrich, Count Palatinate and later Prince Elector, about 1531.

1563	Prince Elector Friedrich III imposes Calvinism. The Heidelberg Catechism becomes the textbook of the reformed faith.
1608-10	Prince Elector Friedrich IV is the leader of the Protestant "Union".
1610	Prince Elector Friedrich V has the famous Schlossgarten ("castle garden") or Hortus Palatinus built, as well as the Englischer Bau ("English Building") and the Elisabethentor (gate) built.
1619	The Protestant citizens in Bohemia elect Friedrich V as their king. In 1620 he loses the "Battle of the White Mountain" against the Emperor's army, and thus also his titles as King and Prince Elector.
1622	The Imperial general Tilly conquers the town and castle of Heidelberg.
1623	The famous "Palatinate Library" is carried off by imperial troops as war booty. Duke Maximilian of Bavaria rules the Palatinate until 1649, with a short interruption of Swedish rule in 1633/34. Warfare robs the state of three-quarters of its population.
1649	Peace of Westphalia: the Upper Palatinate and the old title of Elector fall to Bavaria, but an eighth position of Elector is created for the Palatinate. Prince Elector Karl Ludwig has the castle and the university rebuilt and grants religious freedom to the Lutherans. Flemings, Walloons, Huguenots, Waldenese, and Swiss settle in the Palatinate.
1685	The Palatinate-Simmern line dies out with Prince Elector Karl II and is succeeded by the Palatinate-Neuburg line. King Louis XIV of France raises a claim to the inheritance on behalf of his sister-in-law Liselotte of the Palatinate, but without her consent. Liselotte is married to Louis' brother, and Louis' intention is that the Palatinate should fall to France.
1688/89	During the War of the Palatinate Succession, French troops capture Heidelberg and, before withdrawing, destroy the castle and the town as well as villages and towns in the Rhine plains.
1693	King Louis' troops besiege Heidelberg again, blow up all the fortifications and burn the town to the ground. Even the tombs of the Princes Elector are plundered and destroyed.
1697 onwards	The inhabitants of Heidelberg return to the town and start rebuilding it out of the rubble.
1720	Disputes over religion between the ruling Catholic house and the Evangelical population over the Heiliggeistkirche lead to the transfer of the princes' residence to Mannheim.

1742-99	Prince Elector Karl Theodor promotes trade and industry, has the Alte Brücke ("old bridge") built, and starts work on rebuilding the castle. The Karlstor gate is erected as a triumphal arch in his honour.
1764	During the reconstruction work, lightning destroys further castle buildings and work has to be stopped.
1803	The Imperial Deputation Decree awards Heidelberg to the Grand Duchy of Baden. Karl Friedrich immediately re-establishes the university and gives it the name of the two founders "Ruperta Carola", which it still bears today:.
1810 onwards	The French emigré Charles Count of Graimberg starts on his life's work: conservation of the castle ruins and the construction of a historic collection or museum.
1815	The Tsar of Russia, the Emperor of Austria, and the King of Prussia meet in Heidelberg and form their "Holy Alliance" against Napoleon, the In their honour the castle ruins are illuminated by an enormous wood fire.
1840	Opening of the railway line from Mannheim to Heidelberg and of the old station on the site of the present-day Mengler building.
1848	A conference in Heidelberg passes a resolution calling for a German National Assembly to meet in Frankfurt.
1860	Castle and bridge lit up by "Bengal fire" for the first time.
1920-33	Prominent teachers of medicine (Czerny, Erb, Krehl) and psychology (Rohde, Weber, Gundolf) lecture in Heidelberg.
1945	Courageous Heidelberg citizens succeed at the last moment in handing the city over unscathed to the American military command. It becomes the headquarters for the main military administration departments for the American armed forces in Europe. The university is re-opened on the initiative of the medical professor Karl H. Bauer and the philosopher Karl Jaspers.
1955	The present-day mainline railway station is ceremonially opened.
1978	The Hauptstrasse (main street) is turned into a pedestrian precinct. The city starts work on an extensive modernisation of its old central area.
1980	The Stadthalle ("municipal hall") is opened as a congress centre.

Heidelberg Castle

The view from the north bank of the Neckar, or indeed from the road on the hill above it, the Philosophenweg, arouses curiosity in the world-famous ruins on the Jettenbühl, the narrow mountain terrace above the roofs of the Old Town. It is also readily understandable that, with the invention of firearms, the position of the old castle became strategically less tenable, even with walls up to 7 metres thick confronting the enemy. A number of paths, some of them steep, lead out of the Old Town to the Schlossgarten or offer a ten-minute climb to the fateful sandstone walls of the ruins; the modernised mountain railway takes you there in even less time.

Leaving either the railway halt or the bus-park, the visitor can reach the inner courtyard of the castle with hardly any further climbing. This is the centre of the imposing complex of buildings on which the Princes Electors caused work to be done over a period of three centuries. The stores and workshops, and the palaces, bear witness to the life-style of the lords of this castle in the period from 1400 to 1620 AD, which is when all this was built. The empty window-openings of the destroyed castle buildings give the visitor an entrancing picture of culture and impermanence, of history and of Nature. This two-voiced harmony, originating in the destruction firstly in the War of the Palatinate Succession and then by a stroke of lightning in 1764, was in danger of being lost for ever in the second half of the last century. Efforts were made at the time to rebuild the ruins completely, which would have led to forgery on a grand scale. The danger today comes from the atmospheric pollution which is attacking the richly adorned façades so heavily. As a result, only very few original sculptures are still to be found on the outer frontage.

It strikes the eye at once that the castle did not arise from any uniform constructional plan, and that there is no common building line nor any unifying building style. To the west and the south the dominant element is the very plain Gothic structures, to the north and the east it is the sumptuous and massive stone walls of the magnificent Renaissance palace with its rich decoration of sculptured figures. Taken all together, they form a back-drop of indescribable charm, especially for the open-air stage performances which draw thousands of visitors from all over Germany and all over the world.

Enquiries at the castle ticket office, tel. 538414 or the Castle administrative office, tel.: 53840. Castle courtyard and Großes Faß ("Big Barrel") open: 8 a.m. to 5.30 p.m. Free entrance to Castle courtyard and Großes Faß from 5.30 p.m. to 6 p.m. Conducted tours through the interior of the Castle: ticket office in courtyard. Apothekenmuseum ("Apothecaries' Museum") in the Ottheinrichsbau in the Castle, tel.: 25880, opening hours: daily 10 a.m. to 5.30 p.m.

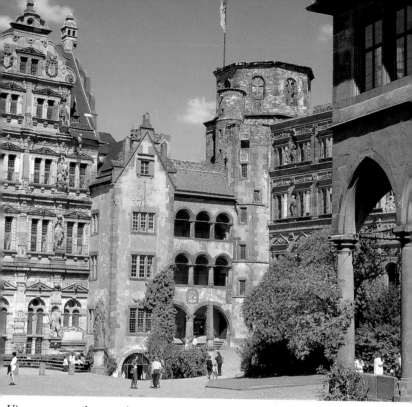

View across the castle courtyard with the well house (foreground), the Ottheinrichsbau (centre), and the Hall of Mirrors. Between them is the Clock Tower.

Ruprechtsbau (King Ruprecht's Building)

This simple home, on the right-hand side of the gateway tower, was built by Prince Elector Ruprecht III from 1400 onwards following his election as King of Germany. In those days the walls were plastered, and then decorated with paintings, and smooth wall surfaces are of course the most suitable kind for this purpose. The only three-dimensional decoration consists of two stone pictures and the key-stone above the entrance, a masterful and legendary piece of Gothic sculpture: two twin-like angels hold a wreath of flowers surrounding a pair of compasses. As the legend goes, the charming twin boys came almost every day to visit their father, the master builder, at his work. Shortly before the building work was completed, they met their deaths in a fall from the scaffolding. The despairing father wove them a funeral wreath of white roses every day, and was unable to finish the building work. Then, one night, his sons appeared before him in a dream as angels, and next morning he found next to his bed fresh and fragrant flowers, blossoms which the night before he had seen withering on the

grave; the white roses had changed into red ones. The master-craftsman set himself at once to his work and created the magnificent keystone depicting his boys, the wreath of roses, and the compasses as the symbol of his profession.

The stone picture on the left, which was originally painted in colours, originates from the time of the building and shows the imperial eagle as a symbol of Ruprecht's kingly title. In its claws it holds the coat-of-arms of the prince-elector family, the Palatinate lion and the Bavarian diamond-pattern. The Renaissance picture, also decorated with coats-of-arms, bears an inscription to remind the onlooker of the renovation of the building under Prince Elector Ludwig V (1508-1544), the great architect of the castle.

Frauenzimmerbau (women's quarters)

This is in the same group of buildings as the Ruprechtsbau and is separated from it by the open space in front of the library. Today only the ground floor is preserved, which is the Königssaal ("King's Hall"): 34 metres long, 16.7 wide, and 7.4 high, it is the largest single room in the castle. It was dedicated in 1534, and served as the scene of noble ceremonial occasions until it lost this position to the newer reception rooms in the Gläserner Saalbau ("Glass Hall") and Ottheinrichsbau. It was then demoted to become a tournament-ground for knightly contests, and later a sculptor's workshop with other workshops for coopers and farriers. In order that they might work unaffected by the weather, Karl Theodor had those walls which were still standing in what had once been the upper floor demolished, and the Hall was simply roofed over. On the occasion of the 400th anniversary of its construction, the Königssaal was renovated from top to bottom and today provides space for nearly 500 visitors on gala occasions and for theatre performances. The ladies of the court once lived in the two plain and simple upper storeys, hence the name; the heavily vaulted lower floor housed the wine-cellar. The roof and the upper floors were badly damaged in the Thirty Years War, hastily repaired, and then totally destroyed in the War of Succession - never to be rebuilt again.

Library

After Ludwig V had had the mighty west wall, also called the Stückgarten, built, he used the outer bailey, which now had no further importance, for the construction of a library building between Ruprechtsbau and Frauenzimmerbau. He based two of its outer walls on the inner and outer castle walls, and thus took the first step in extending living accommodation beyond the confines of the medieval castle. The new building stood on a square plan, and its main function was to provide a home for the private library of the Princes Elector. (At the time this building was built, the famous Palatine Library was already spreading out onto the galleries of the Heiliggeistkirche.) Its mighty surrounding walls, 3 metres thick at the base and still 1.5 metres thick in the upper storey, indicate that the Prince-Elector's mint and his art gallery were also housed here.

...thic oriole window the Library building of the castle of ...e Princes Elector.

The first floor was completely filled just with the library hall, which had a 6.6 metre high star vault supported by a central pillar. Today, an attractive Gothic oriole window in the second floor forms the only decoration of the building on the side facing the castle courtyard, but the consoles and beam holes of the two wooden galleries which used to give the façade a livelier appearance are still visible.

Other Ludwig V buildings

Where the castle ticket office now stands used to be the room for the soldiers on guard duty, and bordering that was the well hall with a 16-metre deep well, fed by spring water from the area of the Königstuhl hills. The pillars are in one piece (monoliths) and are the oldest structural parts of the castle. They were taken from the castle of Charlemagne in Ingelheim, which was than already a ruin, but they could be vastly older - probably of Roman origin.

The workshops and stores adjoin this building to the east. They include the bake-house and the slaughter-house, as well as the main kitchens, which remained roofless after the destructions of the War of Succession.

The adjoining Ludwigsbau demonstrates Ludwig attitude of mind as a builder, always preferring the necessary and the practical to anything smacking of prestige. His residential building dates from 1524, and was built in the simplest possible style, initially on three floors. The coat-of-arms above the entrance door is the only decorative element in the structure. Built on the foundation walls of the building that preceded it, the palace at that time stretched just as far to the north as to the south, so that the staircase tower was more or less in the middle. After all the great wars the building was hastily repaired, but like the neighbouring palaces of Ottheinrich and Friedrich II it fell victim to the stroke of lightning in 1764.

Gläserner Saalbau (Glass Hall)

With this building, built under Ludwig V's successor, the world-traveller Friedrich II, the transition was made from the Gothic style to that of the Renaissance. Its arcaded walks, the staircase tower on the right and the slender, projecting side-wing with the sun-dial and the vaulted gable demonstrate a successful mixture of both styles of architecture. The eastern half of the palace is concealed by the more recent Ottheinrichsbau. The building itself takes its name from the banqueting hall on the upper floor, the north wall of which was clad with Venetian glass, an enormous luxury in those days. The conflagration that followed the stroke of lightning in 1764 lasted for three days and took its greatest toll on this palace. The wooden ceilings offered little resistance, so that afterwards only the outer walls were left. On the courtyard side they are decorated with the coats-of-arms of Friedrich II and his consort. The middle one shows the imperial apple symbol between the Palatinate lion and the Bavarian diamond-pattern. The Emperor Karl V had awarded these arms at the Prince Elector's ascent to the throne to indicate his rank as Arch-Marshal of the Empire. The number 1549 marks the year in which the palace was completed. The arms of his consort, Princess Dorothea of Denmark, is divided into two and, like those of Friedrich, used to be gilded and decorated in magnificent colours. A simple plate at the entrance commemorates the

Romantic fountain in the Castle courtyard.

Count of Graimberg, who made the preservation of the ruined castle his life's work and lived for many years in the well-preserved oriole rooms as its Lord Warden.

The Ottheinrichsbau

Friedrich II ("Friedrich the Wise") was succeeded in 1556 by Otto Heinrich. Although he was only to rule for three years, he is one of the most important of the Princes Elector. He led his nation into the Reformation, and had the artistically most significant palace within the castle built, the Ottheinrichsbau. Its harmoniously designed and richly decorated façade facing the castle courtyard is regarded as the most magnificent example of German Renaissance architecture. When Otto Heinrich took over the government, all he found was a narrow gap between the Ludwigsbau and the Gläserner Saalbau, so he immediately had the north wing of the Ludwigsbau torn down, as far as the staircase tower, so that he had a space 31.5 metres wide available and could integrate the two staircase towers of the adjoining buildings. It can still be seen today, from the coarse masonry of the

The magnificent renaissance façades of the Friedrichsbau and the

...einrichsbau, with the Hall of Mirrors and the Clock Tower between them.

plinth, that the Ludwigsbau in those days would have stretched about as far as to the doorway of the Ottheinrichsbau.

Broad cornices delineate the three floors, which are of different heights, and pilasters and half-columns modelled on Greek architecture divide each of them into five areas. Whilst the upper floors were probably designed to be residential rooms for the prince-elector family, the elevated ground floor served primarily as a magnificent banqueting hall, which also bore the name of Kaisersaal (Emperor's Hall) following the visit of Maximilian II in 1570.

The doorway rises like a triumphal arch over the open staircase flanked by two figures of Atlas on imposing pedestals. The inscription over the arched gateway immortalises Otto Heinrich's titles:

"Ott Hainrich von Gottes gnaden Pfaltzngraf bei Rhein
Des heyligen Römischen Reichs Ertzdruchses und Churfürst,
Hertzog in Nidern und Obern Baiern."

(Ottheinrich, by the Grace of God Count Palatinate on the Rhine, Arch-Marshal and Prince Elector of the Holy Roman Empire, Duke of Lower and Upper Bavaria.)

Above it we can discern the coat-of-arms of the art-obsessed ruler and a medallion bearing his portrait.

The principal figures in the centre of the fenestration are all equally large, although the ceiling-heights are different. From left to right, on the ground floor, they represent the heroes of the Old Testament (Joshua, Samson, Hercules, and David), above them the five Virtues (Strength, Faith, Love, Hope, and Justice), and the gods of antiquity in the upper part of the façade named after the major planets, the sun and the moon (Saturn, Mars, Venus, Mercury, Luna, and above them Sol and Jupiter, who used to decorate the gable frames). The imposing total impression of the façade is only slightly reduced by the workmanship on the statues, which is not always of the best quality, and the simple verses on the pedestals of the figures on the ground floor.

After the great fire of 1764, all that was left were the outer walls and four attractive stone door surrounds on the ground floor, which was provided with an emergency roof. The empty window-openings on the upper floor, however, and the overall view which now forms a square, now permit the magnificent façade to make an even more impressive appearance than did the complete palace.

The Friedrichsbau

In the days when Friedrich IV was on this throne, there was initially no space available for construction anywhere around the castle courtyard. For this purpose the Chapel of Prince Elector Ruprecht I, dedicated in 1346, had to be pulled down (it was close to collapse anyway, although it had only just before been restored). The new building line was extended by also removing the neighbouring tower which had been the main town entrance to Heidelberg. At the lowest point in the courtyard a relatively narrow but still prestigious

Friedrichsbau: 16 elegant statues of the Princes decorate the courtyard façade of the palace of the Princes Elector. The Castle Chapel is on the ground floor.

building could now be built. It was principally required to house the castle chapel, as the Latin inscription explains (translated): "Friedrich, Count Palatinate on the Rhine and Prince Elector of the Holy Roman Empire, Duke of Bavaria, ordered the building of this palace for the maintenance of divine services and to be pleasant living quarters, decorated with many portraits of his ancestors. In this Year of Our Lord 1607." Because the space was cramped, the horizontal and vertical divisions of the façade do not have such an impact as on the Ottheinrichsbau, 50 years older, upon which it was modelled. On the other hand, as a result the mighty statues of the princes, which seem to be almost bursting out of their niches, appear all the more monumental. In the upper row are the princely ancestors of the Wittelsbach dynasty, from the left: the Emperor Charlemagne, Otto von Wittelsbach (first Duke of Bavaria), Ludwig I (the first Wittelsbach Count Palatinate), and Rudolf I (of the main family line, first Count Palatinate of the elector line). Below them appear Wittelsbach emperors and kings: Ludwig the Bavarian (Emperor, and Rudolf's brother), King Ruprecht I of the Palatinate, King Otto of Hungary, and King Christoph of Denmark; Ruprecht I (who founded the University), Friedrich I ("the Victorious"), and Otto Heinrich (who built the adjacent palace). Between the arched windows of the castle chapel, we can see, finally, the immediate predecessors in office from the Palatinate Simmern line, Friedrich III ("the Pious"), Ludwig VI, Johann Casimir (who built the "barrel" building), and, last of all, the builder of this building himself. The standing statues were replaced by good reproductions during the renovation of the building in 1897-1900. The originals, by the sculptor

Prince Elector Friedrich V as King of Bohemia, painted in 1634 by Gerard van Honthorst (1592-1656).

The Castle courtyard in the 17th century, on the left of the Women's Building, the Friedrich Building, the Hall of Mirrors Building, on the right of the staircase are the Ludwig Building and the domestic buildings (engraved by U. Kraus). ➜

Sebastian Götz from Chur, are housed under cover in the interior of the building. The crossways structures in the attic floor have a very pleasing effect, crowned by representations of spring and summer and between them Justitia, Goddess of Justice.

A diary belonging to Friedrich IV has been preserved which includes the entry for 9th July 1598: "Gestern voll gewest" ("Yesterday a skinful"), the title of a drinking song which still enjoys great popularity in Heidelberg; the refrain can be roughly translated thus: "Prince Friedrich of the Palatinate rolled furiously around in bed, Contrary to all etiquette he roared at the top of his voice, How did I get back to my nest yesterday? Seems I'd had a skinful again."

On the other hand, the youthful Prince Elector brought the Palatinate into the centre of the German Reformation movement, and from 1608 to 1610 was the leader of the Protestant Union, but then died at the early age of 36.

The footpath from the Friedrichsbau leads down to the Grosser Fass ("big barrel"), to which we will devote more time when we view the interior. Instead, we will now walk along passage-way under the cross-vaulting, passing one of the doors to the castle chapel, to reach the panorama terrace.

On the great belvedere terrace

On the left, the steep path up from the town via the Burgweg opens out onto this terrace. The terrace itself was created as a belvedere, or panorama-terrace, under Friedrich IV, who had his predecessor's barbican tower extended and added the terrace above it. From here we can enjoy a unique view across the higgeldy-piggeldy roofs of the Old Town, dominated by the Heiliggeistkirche, the River Neckar with the Alte Brücke built under Karl Theodor, the wooded slopes of the Heiligenberg, and beyond that to the densely populated upper Rhine plain with the loops of the Neckar meandering away across it. As one season gives way to the next, and darkness closes in, the impressions gained from up here change in a wonderful way, so that visitors who come here often are constantly offered new delights.

The Princes Elector had the Grosse Batterie built in front of the terrace as a protective wall, the eastern end of which forms the corner

bastion of the arsenal. Only the foundation walls of this are preserved, but it made the north-eastern circular tower superfluous as a defensive structure. It was therefore converted by building octagonal storeys upon it for residential purposes, topped by a great bell (about 1550), since when it has been called the Glockenturm ("bell tower"). After the Thirty Years War, Prince Elector Karl had Friedrich IV's Ballhaus demolished; we today would call it a sports centre. In its place he had the mighty Karlsschanze built in 1681, which with the Karlsturm in front of it gave added protection to the north-east corner, and further gun emplacements several storeys in height at the foot of the Dicker Turm ("Fat Tower").

A glance at the Friedrichsbau shows that it possesses not only the splendid courtyard façade but also a magnificent show-piece side facing the town, on which the features typical of the Renaissance have an even clearer and more harmonious effect. It is flanked by the plain and unadorned external walls of the Gläserner Saalbau and the Frauenzimmerbau. The western end is formed by Johann Casimir's Fassbau ("barrel building"), which after only one upper floor finishes with a flat roof. In this way it let light and air into the upper floors of the Frauenzimmerbau and could also be used as a terrace.

Always a point of attraction for visitors is the depression in one of the sandstone paving stones which looks like the impression made by a boot. During one of the fires, a knight is supposed to have jumped out of one of the upper windows in full armour. Legend has it that he survived unscathed, leaving just his boot-print behind.

Grosses Fass (Big Barrel)

The entrance fee to the castle courtyard includes a visit to see the Big Barrel, which no visitor will want to miss. It is after all the biggest wooden barrel in the world ever to have been filled with wine. Prince Elector Johann Casimir had the vaulted cellar equipped with a barrel holding about 125,000 litres, which Karl Ludwig had replaced in the 17th century with an even bigger one (195,000 litres). Finally, under Karl Theodor, the present-day barrel was constructed in 1751 from 130 oak tree-trunks; it can hold 221,725 litres (over 48,000 Imperial or 58,000 US gallons), and is 8.5 metres across and 7 metres high, with a dance-floor on top. A baroque plaque bears the initials of Prince Karl Theodor.

On the wall opposite is a statue on a plinth representing the dwarf Perkeo. He came from South Tyrol, could reputedly hold a lot of drink, and served as court jester and Keeper of the Vat under Karl Philipp (1716-42). His name is supposed to have come from his habitual reply to the question whether he would like one more beaker of wine to drink: "Perche no?" - "Why not?". Tradition has it that Perkeo died as a result of being talked into drinking a glass of water. He is to this day the symbol of the Carnival in Heidelberg and the enjoyment of life

Karl Theodor's famous "Big Barrel", decorated with his initials, can hold almost 220,000 litres. In front of it is a statue of the dwarf Perke, By Appointment Guardian of the Barrel and Court Jester to the Princes Elector.

23

typical of the Palatinate. He is said to have invented the "clock" hanging next to his statue, the ring of which has been pulled by innumerable visitors from all over the world.

The object that strikes the eye first, apart from the gigantic cooper's tools, is an old piece of water-pipe. This is the remains of a pump mechanism by which wine was pumped out of the Grosser Fass into the pump-room above it. This was on the same level as the Königssaal, so that guests could be plied with wine without the servants constantly having to run up and down stairs. The castle cellars were stocked with a good 700,000 litres of wine, and the drink-happy inhabitants and their guests are reputed to have had a daily consumption of almost 2,000 litres.

Tour of the interior

This tours starts opposite the castle ticket office, in the Ruprechtsbau (circa 1400 AD), the oldest still preserved building. The two main rooms on the ground floor are the same size, both about 8 metres high, and are topped by a cross-vaulting with a keystone in the form of Ruprecht's coat-of-arms. Models show the castle as it was before and after its destruction. A family tree of the Wittelsbachers, a number of glass display cases showing archaeological finds and a Renaissance fire place of great quality complete the furnishings. The latter came from Friedrich II's Gläserner Saalbau and bears the date of 1546.

Gloomy passageways lead through the ruins of the library building to the Königssaal, once located in the lower floor of the former Frauenzimmerbau. It can once again be seen in all its splendour when serving as a ceremonial hall for receptions, such as that in 1979 when a daughter of Heidelberg, Silvia Sommerlath, visited her home town as Queen Silvia of Sweden and was honoured with a State reception. In inclement weather it provides a room for the performance of castle concerts and plays. The portraits of the Princes Elector remind the

The Königs-saal ("King's Hall") ➤

Model of the Castle prior to 1689.

The famous dwarf Perkeo, court fool and wine-loving guardian of the Great Vat (by A. v. d. Werff).

onlooker of its regal past in the same way as the remains of the wine-pump in the neighbouring ground floor room in the Grosser Fass building.

All that remains of the Gläserner Saalbau are the external walls with their massive pilaster columns and the rooms of the projecting

Corridor on the courtyard side of the first floor of the Friedrich Building with precious wooden ceiling and doors.

Torbau (gatehouse) in which von Graimberg lived. A doorway leads into the magnificent Friedrichsbau, the building best preserved despite all the miseries of past centuries and reconstructed, between 1897 and 1900, with great thoroughness and expertise by Professor Karl Schäfer. The two upper floors originally served as accommoda-

The splendour of the hallway on the second floor of the Friedrichs bau, leading to the living accomodation of the Prince Elector and his family.

ion for the princes, but nothing of the interior has been preserved. Nevertheless, the original statues of the princes by Sebastian Götz which once graced the façade are still certainly worth seeing. The details of clothing and armour are so intricately sculpted in stone that one can make out every buckle and every loop. On the other hand, the ceiling decoration, the floors, and the door claddings are copied more in the style of the Renaissance, as are the tiled stoves, the iron grate back-plates, and the few pieces of furniture which have been brought here from various museums.

One original part that has been preserved, however, is the ground floor of the Friedrichsbau, which is completely taken up by the castle chapel. Originally designed to be very plain and simple, in the Calvinist style, when the Residence passed into the Pfalz-Neuburg family in 1685 the altar and the private stalls of the Princes were added in the baroque style. Above the altar, Prince Elector Jan Wilhelm has eternalised himself and his consort, a daughter of the House of Medici and of the Grand Duke of Tuscany, in the reproduction of their coats-of-arms. There are also some interesting coats-of-arms on the statue of King Christoph of Denmark, which include both those of the Scandinavian countries and those of the Wittelsbach lands which he inherited. We should note one particular detail on Prince Elector Johann Casimir, who built the Vat Cellar: he is wearing the English Order of the Garter, worn as custom dictates below the knee, and which was granted to him and later to Friedrich V alone among all the Princes Elector. No church service has been held in the chapel since 1804, yet it is still popular today for other ceremonies, particularly weddings.

Electoral drawing room in the Friedrich Building with Nuremberg tiled stove, precious door frames and moulded ceilings.

The Apothecaries' Museum

The German Apothecaries' Museum presents a unique collection of accoutrements, laboratory equipment, containers, pharmaceuticals, written documents, and books dealing with the field of medicine from the 16th to the 19th century. This is the most extensive exhibition of its kind in the world, and is not only of interest for those with medical training. It has been given a particularly fitting home in the lower floor of the Ludwigsbau, and in the Apothekenturm ("Apothecaries' Tower"). The ground floor of the Ottheinrichsbau is used by its owner, the federal State of Baden-Württemberg, for exhibitions of modern art.

German Apothecaries' Museum in the Castle, with dispensary equipment from earlier centuries.

The massive gate-tower defends the entrance to the Castle courtyard.

Gatehouse and moat

Since it was built by Ludwig V, the gatehouse has served to protect the main entrance and as a "Luginsland" - in the dialect, a watch-tower providing a view over a wide stretch of countryside and of any approaching enemy. 52 metres tall (from the floor of the moat), it was the tallest building in the castle. The Warder of the Tower lived on the top floor, and at the same time looked after the great clock. The former steep pitched roof above it fell victim to the War of Succession, and was replaced around 1718 by the present-day roof. The bulky tower

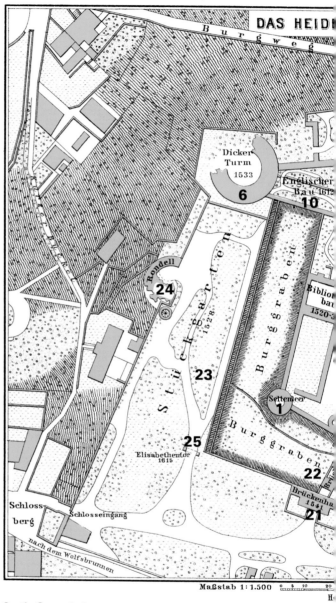

Maßstab 1:1.500

Castle Ground-plan

1 Prison Tower "Seldom Empty" ("Seltenleer")
2 Gate Tower
3 Powder Tower ("Krautturm")
4 Apothecary's Tower
5 Bell Tower
6 Thick Tower
7 Ruprecht Building
8 Library Building
9 Bower (King's Hall)
10 English Building
11 Wine Barrel Building
12 Friedrich Building
13 Great Castle Terrace ("Altan")
14 Arsenal
15 Hall of Mirrors Building

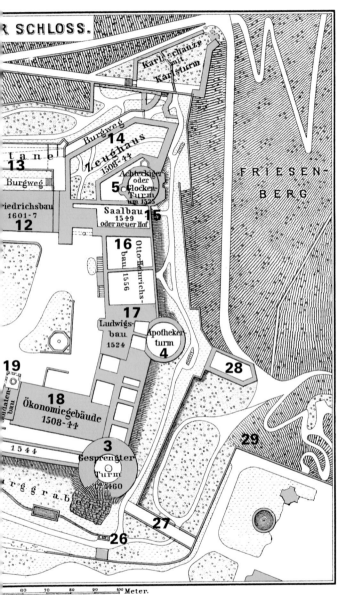

FRIESEN-
BERG

13

ane

Burgweg

14 Zeughaus 1508-44

5 Achteckiger oder Glocken-Turm um 1525

Burgweg

riedrichsbau 1601-7
12

Saalbau 1549 oder neuer Hof
15

16 Ottoheinrichs-bau 1556

17 Ludwigs-bau 1524

Apotheken-turm
4

28

19

oldaten-bau

18 Ökonomiegebäude 1508-44

1544

29

3 Gesprengter Turm um 1460

rggraben

27

26

60   70   80   90   100 Meter.

n.König.

31

was, however, the only structure to have withstood the destructive intention of the "Roi Soleil" with only slight damage.

The entrance itself was protected by four gates and a portcullis. In the central vaulted roof the opening can be seen through which the soldiers on guard-duty could pull anyone up who had been entrapped. An unusual, sharp-cornered protuberance can be seen on one of the heavy iron rings on one of the doors, and this is the origin of the legend of the "witch's bite": The owner, in an off-hand moment, had promised the castle to anyone who could bite through the ring. A witch applied all her magic powers and still only managed to bite into it, as one can still see today.

Underneath the entrance is a high, vaulted room which was formerly used as a dungeon; a prisoner would be let down into it on a rope or with a ladder. As additional defence for the entrance there was a drawbridge located directly in front of the tower which, like the portcullis, was operated from the first floor. On its outer face is the only decoration on this very utilitarian building: two sentries, the Torriesen ("gate giants"), and between them two lions bearing an escutcheon which today has no coat-of-arms on it. This was probably made of silver and has not been seen since the War of Succession. The whole bridge used to have a black-and-white superstructure leading to the bridge-house on the other side of the moat, which is almost 20 metres deep. In front of this, in turn, there used to be a smaller moat which was likewise defended by a drawbridge and had a side entrance with a narrow plank bridge for people on foot. The vaulted arch opposite formed part of the outer defences and was put up in 1619 during the course of the laying out of the "Palatinate Garden" carrying its upper terrace. It provided accommodation for all kinds of equipment and wagons.

Stückgarten (gun garden)

Round to the right, we can now follow the moat which Ludwig V had reinforced on its inward side with a tall and massive stone wall. The entrance to the Stückgarten is formed by the charming Elisabethentor ("Elişabeth's gate"), shaped like a triumphal arch. This, according to tradition, was the one which Prince Elector Friedrich V in 1615 had built in one night for his English royal princess, Elisabeth Stuart. The embankment upon which we are now standing is called the Stückgarten because Friedrich V had it converted into a pleasure-garden for his consort. At the same time, however, it forms a powerful bulwark where guns ("Stücke", or "pieces" of artillery) could be placed. It was built under Ludwig V, who extended the existing south

Western defences with bailey. In the background are the ruins of Friedrich V's buildings, the Englischer Bau, and the thin-walled Festsaal ("banqueting hall") on the massive Dicker Turm ("Fat Tower").

moat along the old bailey wall and had the empty space between the two supporting walls filled in.

The small tower demolished by gunpowder on the other side of the moat, which in places is 25 metres deep, was called Seltenleer ("seldom empty") - it served as a prison. Behind it we can see the

The Elisabethentor as the entrance to the Stückgarten, built in one night as a birthday present for Friedrich V's consort, Elisabeth Stuart.

Ruprechtsbau with its angular staircase tower. The next building, the library, indicates the width of the old bailey, which had lost its defensive function when the west wall was built and which Ludwig was therefore free to build on. This single-storey roofed Frauenzimmerbau, on the other hand, runs along the old building line. The date we can read on the wall here, 1619, was at the same time a fateful year for Friedrich, now 23 years of age. After taking office as Prince Elector at the age of 17, and wanting to impress everybody with enormous building projects, in that year he accepted the position offered to him of King of Bohemia. In the winter of 1619/20 he lost the Battle of the White Mountain against the Emperor's troops, and went down in history as the "Winter King" because after this defeat he was stripped of all his titles and was left to wander through the countryside as a homeless tramp. How wrongly he had estimated the political situation can be seen from the fact that, before moving to Bohemia, he had dismissed his troops and his generals. The Emperor's General, Tilly, therefore had no trouble capturing the defenceless Palatinate, as well as the castle - for the first time in its history.

The Dicker Turm was the only one in Germany, apart from the Eckturm of the Hardenburg castle in the Palatinate, which had such enormous dimensions: an external diameter of 28 metres, walls 7 metres thick all round, and a total height of 40 metres. All the same, the army engineers of the "Roi Soleil" still succeeded in blowing it up. Due to this destruction, the massiveness of the structure is now even more apparent. From the side towards the city, one can see the five rows of coping stones which bore the intermediate wooden ceilings. A sturdy continuous pillar served as a central support for the roof. In order further to reinforce his western wall, Ludwig V had a five-storey "Rondell" built, a semi-circular artillery tower. This linked the level of the western wall with the Dicker Turm and the north tower with passageways and spiral staircases, and
today is partly restored.

A memorial plaque near the Rondell commemorates the visits Goethe made in 1814 and 1815 and his friendship with Marianne von Wilemer, who dedicated the poem to him. We now go back along the main path, past the main gate, and across to the actual castle garden on the eastern side of the site.

In the Castle Garden

We remain at the same level as the entrance and keep over to the left so that we can look at the fortifications on the east side. Certainly one of the most impressive is the Krautturm ("Herb Tower") at the south-east corner, erected back in 1460 as a flanking tower. Gunpowder used to be stored in its basement. It has an external diameter of 24 metres, and the outer walls are up to 6.5 metres thick. At the French troops' second attempt to blow it up in 1693, the colossal structure split into two pieces, one of which slithered as a complete mass into the moat, opening up the unique view into the inside. Although it had first had wooden intermediate floors providing firing positions, Friedrich IV had the vaulted roof built with the central pillar and the octagonal upper floor placed on top if it. The firing slits, the chimney for drawing off the gunpowder fumes, and the rings for supporting the firearms are all still visible. A gun emplacement in line with the

The massive, circular Krautturm, blown up in 1693 to reveal the view of the interior.

*Water playing on Vater Rhein,
the River God.*

JOHANN WOLFGANG
GOETHE
1749—1832

*Goethe memorial
in the Castle gardens.*

tower marks the end of the moat towards the Friesental valley, reinforced by a sharp-cornered emplacement in line with the Apothekenturm.

The lower floors also date from the 15th century, when the lord of the castle considered it necessary to strengthen the eastern flank facing the Friesenberg hill. When a covered defensive strip was built at its foot, the tower lost some of its strategic significance and was then used as accommodation. This included the castle's apothecary shop, which gave the tower its name. To the north comes the plain, unadorned outer side of the Ottheinrichsbau, the magnificent courtyard façade of which is so impressive. The oriole window beyond that belongs to the gable end of the Gläserner Saalbau, which forms a link with the clock-tower beyond it.

The terraces of the castle garden were built under the "Winter King" Friedrich V, who had the castle to the west and north of his residence adapted to suit the taste of his age and the pompous attitude of his court. For this purpose he summoned the French engineer Salomon de Caus, who took charge of the planning and by 1616 had already made a start on the building work. Hundreds of people worked on the gigantic project; they blasted rock, levelled hills, and filled in the space behind the supporting walls, some of which were 20 metres high. Thus a work of art arose from the bare Friesental valley which, if strategically not very clever, was unique and formed a harmonious link with the castle. Numerous flights of steps led up to the five terraces, on which little weirs and charming statues were arranged between the symmetrically laid out flower-beds and exotic stands of timber. The greenhouses of the Orangerie and the Pomeranzgarten could be heated, and in the Grosse Grotte, under the watchful eye of "wild animals", one could look at coral, molluscs, rare stones, and artistic waterfalls. On the narrow side of the fourth terrace, Friedrich had statues larger than life size set up of himself and his consort, and between them were heated bath-houses and fish-breeding basins.

The garden was still far from finished when Friedrich moved off to Bohemia in 1619, but nevertheless it was already enjoying the reputation of a miraculous garden, the eighth wonder of the world, described, lauded, and painted by many contemporaries. 1622 was the first time a battle took place upon it, which partly destroyed it, and it fell visibly into disrepair during the course of the Thirty Years War. After being destroyed totally during the War of Succession it fell into total decay. Karl Friedrich of Baden had it newly laid out in the style of an English park, as we know it today, and as Goethe also came to know it during his visits in 1814/15.

View from the Scheffel terrace across the Old Town of Heidelberg and the Neckar, and beyond that into the broad Rhine plains.

A walk through the Old Town

Before Heidelberg existed, its present-day suburbs of Neuenheim and Bergheim were already well known. At a very early stage it seems likely that not only fishermen but also craftsmen and traders settled close to the ford across the Neckar and enjoyed the protection of the castle. The Old Town came into existence around 1200, with its walls on the western side running along the present-day streets of Grabengasse and Grosse Mantelgasse, on the eastern side from the clock tower along Leyergasse and on the south side along the Zwingerstrasse, whilst the north wall naturally followed the course of the Neckar. Ruprecht II (1390-98) doubled the fortified area of the town by integrating the foregate up to the present-day Sophienstrasse. However, the town needed another 450 years to fill this space up completely, and it was only in 1846 that it took the daring step of building the railway station on the wide open spaces beyond the Sophienstrasse.

In the Middle Ages the citizens tried to make the best possible use of the confined space within the walls by building tall, narrow houses in the Gothic style, so that the houses in each part of the town were built cheek by jowl on tiny plots of land, separated by narrow, twisty

Guided tours: April–October: Daily 10 a.m. in German, Thursday to Sunday 10 a.m. in English. Nov.–March: Saturdays 10 a.m. only in German. Groups meet on the Universitätsplatz. Information from the Verkehrsverein (Tourist Office), tel.: 06221/142211.

40

alleys. Although the town was almost completely burnt down in 1689/93 and only a few old buildings were preserved, the "new" Old Town was rebuilt with only a few exceptions upon the pattern of the old. The citizens, returning after an absence of some years, endeavoured only to rebuild their former properties as quickly and simply as possible in order to have a roof over their heads. Whenever possible they even made use of the old cellars and basements as foundations for the narrow gabled houses. Access was from a passage on one side to an outside staircase on the rear side. In this way the Old Town, although it was only built from 1700 onwards, came to harmonise very well with the old castle, which had not developed any further after about 1620.

Universitätsplatz

The Heidelberg tourist association has prepared a tour through the Old Town and provided all the major buildings with numbers and a brief informative description. We will also start our tour at Universitätsplatz and follow the suggested route.

The old University with its Baroque roof and elegant gateways. In front is the Lion fountain.

Grabengasse runs away east of this square, which marks the transition from the Old Town to the foregate, and is named after the old town moat. Between the Hauptstrasse and the broad Universitätsplatz itself lies the three-storey, Baroque building, the **"Alte Universität"** ❶ (Old University). The bell tower and the clock tower rise above its curving roof. Two gateways with a curving roof line form the only decoration on the building, which Prince Elector Johann Wilhelm had built in 1712-28 from plans by Johann Breunig. The

The Aula (assembly hall) of the old University, with elaborate wall and ceiling decorations dating from the 19th century.

university chancellor's offices are accommodated here, as well as the prestigious Aula (assembly hall), which was given a luxurious, wooden wainscoting with wall-paintings on the occasion of the 500th anniversary of the foundation of the university.

After Pope Urban VI had permitted Prince Elector Ruprecht I to found a university, its teaching rooms were originally scattered all over the town. Its first chancellor was the famous Magister Marilius from Inghen. Ruprecht endowed it with a constitution which was read out in the Heiliggeistkirche on 1st November every year and confirmed by a citizens' oath. It assured the students, teachers, book-sellers, and clerks freedom of passage as well as exemption from excise and taxes. Right from the first year 500 students found their way to Heidelberg, and 10 short years later the first university building stood on the site still called Alte Universität. Its immediate predecessor had been the Collegium Casimirianum, built in 1591 under Johann Casimir. A memorial plaque in the staircase commemorates him.

During the Wars of Religion, and the havoc of warfare in general in the 17th and 18th centuries, the university's activities were greatly reduced, and it had to be re-founded in 1805 by the Count Marcher Karl Friedrich of Baden before it could regain its former significance, and still today bears the name "Ruperto Carola", after the two founders, Ruprecht and Karl (Friedrich).

There are now almost 30,000 students registered in Heidelberg, divided among 9 faculties. A large part of the university has been transferred to the new site of Neuenheimer Feld, leaving only the sciences in their lecture theatres and institute buildings in the Old Town. Nevertheless, it is here, the square in front of the Alte Universität, that forms Heidelberg's main meeting place, with young people in debate, street musicians, international tourism, and students hurrying past. In its midst the Palatinate Lion keeps watch over the bowl of the fountain, but even he no longer seems to glare into it as fiercely as in the days of the "great nobility". The Augustinergasse at the back of the Alte Universität recalls the Augustinian monastery that used to occupy the present-day Universitätsplatz and which was destroyed in 1693 with the rest of the town. This is where Martin Luther, on 26th April 1518, presented the justification for his teaching to the General Chapter of his Order. In the Augustinergasse one can find the entrance to the historic Studentenkarzer ("student's dungeon") in the former Pedellenhaus, one of the main attractions for students. It served from 1712 to 1914 as a prison for students, over whom the university administration had legal sovereignty. Violations of public order (mainly drunkenness, gross misbehaviour, breaches of the night-time peace, or preferably a combination of all three) were punished with up to two weeks in prison, and if resistance was offered against the forces of the State this often ran to four weeks. Many of the undergraduates regarded such crimes as a "Kavaliersdelikt" - a mere "gentleman's offence" which they expected to be allowed to get away with - and just as much part of the degree course as the final examination. It was only for the first two or three days that they were "starved" on bread and water, and after that they were allowed to have meals sent in from outside, receive visits from fellow-prisoners, and even attend lectures. Many generations of students have immortalised themselves in their "cells" with water-colour and candle-soot, giving the cells names like "Grand Hotel" and "Sanssouci" (after the Prussian palace in Potsdam). In an extension of the Augustinergasse southwards, on the wall of a Baroque building, we find a plaque commemorating Nadler, the local-dialect poet who was born here.

The plain and simple building on the south side of "Uniplatz" is called "Neue Universität", and is dedicated "To the living spirit". It was built with funds handed over to the University in 1928 from a donation campaign in the United States. The only decoration on the extensive three-winged building is a statue of Pallas Athene, Goddess of Wisdom, above the entrance. The inscription was altered by the Nazis to read "To the German spirit", but in 1945 the original wording was restored.

The inner courtyard of this building opens to the east. Its south-west corner integrates the **Hexenturm** ("witch's tower") of 1380 **②** which is the only medieval tower to have been preserved. It once served as a women's prison, and was later converted into a memorial to the former students who were killed in the first world war.

The left-hand side of the street includes the former **Jesuitengymnasium** ("Jesuit boys' school") **③**, an extended, plain building which housed the university library during the 19th century.

Climbing a few steps, we reach the Seminarstrasse; exactly opposite is the Ehrenhof ("Court of Honour") in front of the most beautiful Jesuit building, the **"Collegium Academicum" ④**. Founded in 1720 as a seminary, it was intended to serve the Jesuits as a magnet for recruiting new members. After Pope Clement XIV dissolved the Order in 1773 it passed into the possession of the University, and served a variety of functions. Prior to 1808 it housed a Catholic boys' school, between 1826 and 1843 a "mad-house", and from then until 1876 the Surgical and Medical University Clinic. A memorial plaque on the wall of the eastern pavilion commemorates the soldiers of the 110th Grenadier Regiment who were accommodated here from 1881 to 1914, 1,363 of whom fell in the first world war. Later parts of a

Studentenkarzer ("Students' Prison"), Alte Universität, Augustinergasse, tel.: 542334, opening hours: April–Oct. Tues.–Fri. From 10 a.m. to 4 p.m. Closed on Monday, Saturday, Sunday and public Holidays

Custodys cells in the students' prison in the Augustinergasse.

The Witches' Tower (Hexenturm) in the quadrangle of the New University was once part of the city's defences (1380).

school and a students' dormitory were at home here, and now the central University administration office is housed in it.

The attractive three-wing structure directs the eye to the centre of the building, the forward part of which is crowned with round arches and decorated triangular gables pointing upward to the cheerful, elegant roof pinnacles.

East of the Jesuitengymnasium a Palazzo with a touch of the south has pushed its way between the Jesuit buildings; it is the former Court of Justice. Between this and the Jesuitengymnasium we can descend the Schulgasse. We pause for a while in the little square in front of the **Jesuitenkirche** ❺ ("Jesuits' church"), the northern façade of which is decorated with statues of the founder of the Order, Ignatius Loyola. The foundation was laid in 1712, while the whole town still lay in ruins. The first part of the building work based on plans by the Heidelberg architect Breunig, took until 1723, whilst the second phase of building under Rabaliatti was not completed until 1759. The interior has an almost weightless effect and the font by Brandens and the organ gallery by Rabaliatti are worth seeing. The crypt, next to the side entrance on the left, holds the mortal remains of the powerful Prince Elector Friedrich I and members of his family. They were finally laid to rest here after an odyssey through a number of monasteries. The church nowadays houses a museum of sacred art and liturgy.

The western side of the square in front of the church is graced by a beautiful Madonna statue by Brandens, in front of house number Schulgasse 2. Three full storeys, as plain as a barracks, stretch along the Merianstrasse and up the Kettengasse. This gigantic building, after housing a school for many years, is now completely occupied by the University. After examining the Kettengasse frontage, we can now follow the Ingrimstrasse which virtually forms an extension of the Merianstrasse.

Madonna statue near the Jesuits' church.

View into the choir of the Baroque Jesuits' church (1712 - 1759).

In the eastern part of the Old Town

On the way through the typical Old Town alleyways we pass various narrow alleys, which now and again permit a glimpse of the house fronts all squeezed up together. It is easy to imagine what effect the wreaths of burning pitch had when the French soldiers set fire to one block of houses after another in 1693. Chronicles from as long ago as 1265 mention a bath-house in the **Mittelbadgasse** ❻, which we now follow to the left. We can continue our course eastwards by following the Hauptstrasse. When we reach the Rathaus ("town hall"), the pedestrian precinct opens up to the right and leads to the

View across the Kornmarkt to the Castle ruins with the Clock Tower and the 7 metre thick external walls of the Dicker Turm.

Kornmarkt ("corn market") ❼, where one has a fine view up to the magnificent castle ruins. At the forward corner of this there stood, until 1978, Heidelberg's one and only luxury hotel, the "Prinz Carl", in which such famous people stayed during the 19th century as the later Kaisers Wilhelm I and Friedrich III, Bismarck, General von Moltke, and Mark Twain. The building was to have been renovated

*The Kornmarkt
Madonna in front
of the Castle ruins.*

from top to bottom, but then it was discovered that not even the
outer walls were structurally sound. Since then, the sections
possessing historic value have been kept in the south-west corner of
the enlarged square. Because of this change in the relative dimensions, the fountain with the "Kornmarkt-Madonna" now unfortu-
nately no longer marks the middle of the square. This artistic
Baroque statue was created by the sculptor Peter von den Branden
in 1718, under a commission by the Prince Elector. It originally stood
on a column, until the present fountain was finished in 1830. With
the castle wall in the background, this work of art represents a most
attractive objects for painters and photographers.

The corner house at the beginning of Burgweg is called **"Haus
Graimberg"** ❽, as this is where the Castle conservator and founder
of the municipal museum lived. It is still possible to discern the
French inscription, in a window opening, which advertised his
copper engravings.

We can reach the Karlsplatz via the Karlstrasse, formerly called
Kaltes Tal ("Cold Valley"). This square was once upon a time completely occupied by the cloister of the bare-footed Carmelite monks.
After this had lain as heap of rubble for over 100 years, after 1693,
the residents along the Karlstrasse bought the ruins by auction in
1803 and had the site laid out as a public garden.

The modern fountain in the middle of the square is dedicated to the well-known humanist, cosmographer, and Hebraist Sebastian Münster who for his "cosmography" created a wood-cut showing a view of Heidelberg in the 16th century. The fountain, with its sloping elliptical planes and water-arches, symbolises the courses of the planets and with an over-sized globe of the Earth the significance which Man attaches to it.

The castle ruins lower over the southern side of the square, and seem to oppress it. This side, in turn, is dominated by the broad Baroque building, the **Grossherzogliches Palais** ("Palace of the Grand Dukes" ❾. Built in 1717 as accommodation for state officials, it passed into the possession of the Prince Elector in 1768 and initially housed the offices for the state scribes. In the 19th century it was available to the Court of the House of Baden whenever it was in residence in Heidelberg. The Academy of Sciences has occupied it since the 1920's. It has been beautifully restored, and possesses attractive stucco ceilings, cosy corners behind the tiled stoves, wainscoting and fittings, and a terrace garden with pavilion-like side-buildings, all of which is well worth seeing.

Two doors further, on the left, is an interesting Old Town house, the **Mittermaierhaus** ❿. This was built with three wings in the 18th century, but the side wings are built on the rear side towards the garden. Its most famous inhabitant, from 1821 to 1867, was Karl Josef Anton Mittermaier, a legal scholar and politician, whose family continued to own it until 1958. Since then it has served as a student dormitory.

The middle of the northern side of the square is taken up by the equally old Sickingen Palace, more often known nowadays as the **Palais Boisserée** ⓫. The brothers Sulpiz and Melchior Boisserée had rented the building from 1810 to 1819 to house their famous collection of Old German paintings which today can be seen in the Alte Pinakothek in Munich. A second memorial plaque commemorates visits by Goethe, who spent more than two weeks with these art collectors in 1814 and again in 1815. After the art collection had received the acknowledgement of the famous writer, the house became a meeting point for politicians and high society.

We can now follow the Hauptstrasse further eastwards, passing two of the most famous historic student taverns, the "Seppi" and the "Roter Ochsen". Charming little alleyways lead away uphill to the right, the Kisselgasse and the Plankengasse, which once provided the link, with their steep extension the Eselpfad ("Ass Path") between the Herrenmühle mill on the bank of the Neckar and the castle itself. The block of houses between the two alleys is now filled by the University Scientific and Theological Seminary. An attractive Empire gateway in the Kisselgasse was part of an earlier building integrated into the present one.

The Palais Boisserée on the Karlsplatz.

◀ A historic students' tavern: "Sepp'l".

"Zum roten Ochsen".

On the right, the attractive open flight of steps with the Empire grill of **"Haus Buhl"** ⑫ further narrows down the cramped Hauptstrasse. It stands on the property of a former Court Judge. The garden, stretching up almost to the castle, is where Princess Liselotte von der Pfalz once stole cherries. The interior of the house, with its remarkable stairs, reflects the idyllic charm of the Biedermeier age, and is used nowadays by the University as accommodation for official guests.

Exactly opposite perches the simple and unadorned Baroque **"Palais Weimar"** ⑬, encircling an attractive interior courtyard with its single-storey side wing. Built some time after 1700 as the residence of a General, it changed hands many times and in 1921 came into the possession of the Portheim institute for science, which today maintains an anthropological museum in it.

The steep alleyway called "Friesenberg" leads to the castle garden. On the left of it is where the Cistercians from Schönau once owned a monastery where the brothers lived who were studying at the university. After its destruction, the bare-footed Carmelites moved onto the site. In the 18th century their church served as a mausoleum for the Wittelsbach Princes Elector. After Heidelberg had become part of Baden, however, the princely family had the bones of their forefathers transferred to Munich. Only the Jakobsgasse, branching off to the left from the Hauptstrasse, reminds us today of a monastery that once used to cover a large area.

The complex of buildings opposite was built on the site of the Herrenmühle mill, which burnt down in 1972, and was the focus of great attention as a milestone in the process of renovating the town centre. The small facets of the façades and roofs are skilfully linked

The Karlstor at the eastern end of the Old Town. ➤

Palais Weimar, today a museum of anthropology.

Völkerkundemuseum ("Anthropology Museum") Hauptstrasse 235, tel.: 22067, opening hours: Tuesdays to Fridays, 3.00 to 5.00 p.m., Sunday 1.00 to 5.00 p.m.

to the overall appearance of the Old Town. Prior to this, and during the 600 years of its existence, the fortified mill on the bank of the Neckar had developed into a modern industrial mill, before finally being closed down in 1962.

At the **Karlstor**  we reach the eastern end of the Old Town. The town's aldermen laid the foundation stone of this magnificent gateway in 1775 in the presence of Prince Elector Karl Theodor, as a way of paying homage to him. As is not unusual with large projects even today, the cost of building it overshot the original estimates many times over - to the disgruntlement of the citizens. The building was nevertheless completed despite the fact that Karl Theodor had by then already removed his residence to Munich. Three prison rooms were fitted out in the lower and in the upper floor, and two guard-rooms on the ground floor. The classical building, which has a sturdy but at the same time harmonious effect, stands near the exits of two tunnels. Whilst the one to the rear is still used by the railway, the older one in front of it serves as a car tunnel, in order to take some of the load off the streets of the Old Town. It was built in 1859/62, and links the Neckar valley via the Friedrich Ebert Anlage and a second tunnel with the old mainline railway station which dates from 1840.

A weir was built across the Neckar in line with the Karlstor, to prevent floods and to keep the navigable water at a uniform depth. Ships travel from one level to another by means of locks. The lock path also leads across to the north side of the Neckar, where the visitor can walk up the Hirschgasse to Heidelberg's showpiece road, the Philosophenweg.

The road which leads us along the Neckar again in the direction of the city centre is called "Am Hackteufel" - roughly, "the devil with a chopper". The granite blocks projecting out into the river here have been a hazard for many a coxswain, who would blame his clumsiness on powers from below the earth.

At Neckarmünzplatz we find a parking space and an information centre for motor-coaches, and multi-lingual staff to look after tourists. The Leyergasse's western side marks roughly the course of the town wall in the Middle Ages, which used to run from here to the castle fortifications, with the Jakobsviertel district outside. From the Leyergasse we bear right into the Heiliggeistgasse, which leads us the **Schmitthennerhaus** ❻. The writer Adolf Schmitthenner, who was at the same time the parish priest of the Christus and Heiliggeistkirche, lived here in the second half of the 19th century. In addition to his Heidelberg stories and short novels, he became particularly well known for his novel Das deutsche Herz ("The German Heart").

The Mönchgasse which continues on from it is a reminder of the Cistercian monks of Schönau who maintained a small monastery and the mill on the Neckar here prior to the destruction of Heidelberg. While we have the imposing façade of the Heiliggeistkirche in view, our attention is also caught by another, sprawling Baroque building, the **Nebelhaus** ❻. Above its gateway on the right we can see the coat-of-arms of the Court Apothecary, Nebel, dated 1710. The building stands on the site of the old courts of the "Landschaden" of Neckarsteinach. This alley opens out next to the Rathaus into the market square, the centre-point of any town in the Middle Ages.

View across the Marktplatz with the oldest part of the town hall, on which building work started only a short time after the destructions of 1689/93.

Marktplatz (Market Square)

In Heidelberg, its distinctive character comes from two buildings, on the western and the eastern side: the Heiliggeistkirche ("Church of the Holy Ghost"), and the Rathaus ("Town Hall"). The fountain in the middle, the Herkulesbrunnen, looks down with stoic calm on the to-ing and fro-ing at its foot: the market, the students' May Madrigals, the burning of the symbol of winter after the Summer's Day procession, and the young people resting on its steps. The figure of Hercules, produced by H. Charrasky in 1701, is a breathe of Baroque pleasure. In earlier centuries the square was the place where public courts of justice were held and punishments inflicted such as the burning of witches and heretics. It has been handed down to us in old documents that in 1525 "on the market square, of seven the head was struck off, and of three the fingers hewn off." In 1572, Superintendent Sylvanus of Ladenburg was publicly beheaded for siding with Aryans, and in 1812 the robber captain Hölzerlipps and his gang were condemned to death, a punishment which was then carried out on the gallows in front of the western town wall. Until

The Hercules fountain in the Marktplatz.

1740, a Triller, a rotating hanging cage stood next to the fountain. For minor crimes, people were imprisoned in it and exposed to the derisive laughter of their fellow citizens as it twirled around.

The **Rathaus ⓘ** did not grow to its present size until some centuries had run their course. After the preceding building, like nearly all others, had lay in ruins for more than 10 years, and once the citizens had screwed up enough courage work started on removing the rubble and putting up a new building in 1701. The first building was relatively small, and today forms the central part of the market square façade. The coat-of-arms above the balcony door, a piece of decoration boasting magnificent colours and several hundredweight, was produced by the sculptor Charrasky, who also created the figure of Hercules.

The Heiliggeistkirche dominates the centre of the Old Town. A unique feature is the market stalls between the buttresses.

In the south-west corner of the market square, the splendid colours of the coat-of-arms of the Palatinate Princes Elector indicate that the building is the former **Hofapotheke** ("Court Dispensary") ⓲, a Baroque building dating from the period of reconstruction after 1700. It is on this side that the peculiarly ugly gargoyles of the mighty **Heiliggeistkirche** ⓳ look down. In contrast to most other Gothic churches, its façade is designed as one uniform piece, so that neither the choir nor the side-naves can be discerned from outside. This is the largest Gothic church anywhere in the Palati-

nate, and Prince Elector Ruprecht III laid the foundation stone in 1398. 12 years later the choir was built, followed in 1441 by the central nave. Work next started on the tower, 82 metres tall, but this was not finished until 1544. A unique feature is the small shops between the might buttresses; these are mentioned in a document as long ago as 1483. The coat-of-arms of Johann Wilhelm and his consort, a Medici princess, adorns the Hauptstrasse side, indicating that the church in addition to its main function also served as a mausoleum for the princely family; it was also the ceremonial hall for the University.

There are tomb plaques covering four centuries let in to the walls, but the 55 tombs of the Princes Elector were almost completely destroyed in 1693. It was only the tomb of the founder of the church, King Ruprecht I, and his consort, which survived unscathed. In that catastrophic year, many Heidelberg citizens had sought refuge in the church from the plundering and pillaging soldiers of the Roi Soleil, or were driven into it and locked in. The burning roof had already begun to cave in when the French Field-Marshal took pity on the poor people and let them out.

The church is 60 metres long and 20 wide, even though it appears narrower than the choir due to the effect of the rows of columns in the main nave. The nave is, however, much darker, because of the galleries which were built in much later. On the other hand, this did

◄ *Heiliggeistkirche – a view through cramped central nave into the brighter choir.*

Heiliggeistkirche – the physicists' window with biblical texts and the date of the disaster of Hiroshima.

create space for what was in those days the largest collection of books in the world, the famous Bibliotheca Palatina. The donations of a nobleman (1419) and of the Counts Palatinate Ludwig III and, in particular, Otto Heinrich, were augmented by Huldrich Fugger with a store of books weighing 235 hundredweight. These irreplaceable written documents were laid out for general use on the tall, sloping-topped desks with which the galleries were furnished. As a precaution against theft they were fastened with chains and padlocks, but these were ineffective against the arbitrariness of Marshal Tilly and Duke Maximilian of Bavaria. After Heidelberg was captured in 1623, the Emperor's marshal had crates made out of the desks, pews, and chest lids, and the booty hauled off to Rome on 50 wagons. In addition to this, the most valuable library in the western world, the princes' private library and that of the University also disappeared. Today, all but a small proportion is still part of the Papal Library in the Vatican. Some of the manuscripts, mainly in German, were given back at the beginning of the 19th century and are now houses in the Heidelberg University Library, as is the famous Manessische Liederhandschrift, a manuscript of ancient ballads acquired in 1888 and once owned by the Princes Elector. After the church was rebuilt in about 1700, the Catholic and the Reformed Church initially both used it alternately, but in 1705 a wall was built between the nave and the choir. Prince Elector Karl

Heiliggeistkirche – the tomb of King Ruprecht (d. 1410) and his consort.

The choir of the Heiliggeistkirche. The mighty organ is the focus of attention at the church concerts several times a year.

Philipp (1716-42), however, demanded the whole of the church as a mausoleum for his family. The stubbornness of the catholic ruler and the resistance of the Protestant part of the population developed into a struggle which led finally to the Prince Elector transferring his residence to Mannheim. The dividing wall remained, a symbol of Christian intolerance, until 1936. A walk around the top of the tower provides a magnificent view over the Old Town, the Neckar, the castle, and the Königstuhl hills.

On the other side of the Hauptstrasse stands the only private house, **"Haus zum Ritter"** ("The Knight's House") **20**, to have survived the wars of the 17th century without any major damage. The Calvinist Charles Belier had come to Heidelberg as a refugee persecuted for

his religion, and there he had the magnificent Renaissance building erected in 1592. The vaults in the ground floor and the cellar were storage rooms for the wares of the cloth-merchant, which he then set out for sale on the fold-down shutters in the ground floor. The artistically designed façade recalls the famous palace buildings of Otto Heinrich and Friedrich IV, which are about the same age. A particularly pleasing feature is the powerful horizontal and vertical division of the upper and gable floors by strips, half-columns, and pilasters, with symmetrical fenestration and slightly protruding oriole windows. The busts of Otto Heinrich and Friedrich, with their coats-of-arms are located at the base of the second floor, on the right, each supported on the left by an angel. The Beliers' heraldic animal is the ram - belier, in old French. Also printed on the shield is the name Carolus Belier and the date, 1592. The busts one storey lower represent his children. Two of the Latin inscriptions bear witness to the piety of the Huguenots: "si Jehovah non adificet domum, frustra laborant aedificantes eam" (if God does not build the house, the builders work in vain), and, in the uppermost part of the gable, "soli deo gloria" (Glory be to the One God). Between them, however, is the rather slightly more profane message, "persta invicta Venus" (do not weaken, indomitable Venus).

After the destruction of the town in 1693, this house did duty as the town hall for ten years, and from 1703, i.e. for almost 300 years, it has been used as a hotel. A few metres further along the Hauptstrasse, on the corner to Kettengasse, is an appealing Madonna figure in front of the **Medersches Haus ㉑**, another building dating from the 18th century. Another one adorns the corner niche in the **Tratteursches Haus ㉒**, situated on the north side of the Heiliggeistkirche facing the Fischmarkt. The fountain on the wall of the Heiliggeistkirche is the successor of the one which would have been obligatory for a fish market.

← *Renaissance façade of the Hotel "Zum Ritter".*

Shop at the foot of the Heiliggeistkirche.

Baroque decoration on the house of a wealthy citizen: the Fischmarkt Madonna.

Northern part of the Old Town

Hauptstrasse divided the Old Town into two halves even in medieval times, with the side-alleys leading northwards in a herring-bone pattern and southwards towards the town walls. Steingasse now leads from the Heiliggeistkirche straight down to the **Alte Brücke** ("Old Bridge"), via the **Brückentor** ("Bridge gate"), ㉓. From the historic tavern "Zum Hackteufel" there is a magnificent view of the gatehouse, framed by the harmonious house frontages of the alley. The towers were built as part of the medieval town fortification. Together with them, and later a high gatehouse tower near the northern bank, the entrance to the town was secured in those days across a wooden bridge. The connecting building was put up in 1786-88 at the same time as the beautifully curved stone bridge to be found there today, which replaced a chain probably of 8 bridges which kept falling victim to floods or ice-floes. A spiral staircase in the eastern tower leads to the municipal accommodation in the connecting building. The western tower contains three custody cells. Although the side facing the town is of finer workmanship, the north side is the one that is photographed far more often; it catches the imagination with its backdrop of Old Town alleyways, house frontages, and the tower of the Heiliggeistkirche. According to the Latin inscription on the first pillar behind the Brückentor, "The Council and populace of Heidelberg, in all humility, raised a monument to Carl Theodor, the Father of the Palatinate" in 1788. The bas-reliefs on the plinth of the standing statue represent not only the coat-of-arms of the Princes Elector but also important events from the period of his government: the unification of the Palatinate with Bavaria, the 400th anniversary of the University, and the 50th of his government. The Princes are surrounded by representations of the river-gods of the Rhine, the Danube, the Neckar, and the Mosel. A rather newer plaque informs the visitor about the floods of the old days, marking their levels clearly and visibly on the second pillar of the bridge.

The second sculpture, near to the north bank, shows Karl Theodor together with Pallas Athene, the goddess of wisdom. The female figures at the goddess' feet symbolise piety, justice, agriculture, and trade, and the bas-reliefs represent astronomy, architecture, sculpture, and painting - fields of activity which were of particular interest to the Prince Elector.

Today, the oldest of the bridge statues stand in a small square on the north bank, named after the patron saint of bridges, Nepomuk. From 1738 onwards it stood on the second pillar from the north bank in place of the gateway tower of the earlier bridge, which had been destroyed, but when the stone bridge was built it had to make way for Pallas Athene. The stately Baroque sculpture, decorated as it is with numerous angels' heads, shows among other things the lion from the Heidelberg coat-of-arms up on the Dreiberg, protected by the vanguard as a mark of the rank of an Elector.

Gateway of the Old Bridge, with the tower of the Heiliggeistkirche in the background. In the foreground is the statue of Prince Elector Karl Theodor, who had the bridge built.

Returning across the bridge, we can enjoy the view of the picturesque gatehouse and its backdrop. The building to its left was the **Neckar school** ㉔ from 1706 onwards. An earlier building stood here as early as the 16th century. The gateway arch can be clearly recognised, the "Tränktor" through which thirsty cattle were driven down to the Neckar. On the town side one can still see the stone coat-of-arms belonging to the butchers' guild hall, which served at the same time as the slaughterhouse. In the Middle Ages, the mighty Princes Elector's corn-house, stood to the west of the Brückentor. It must have narrowed down the square enormously, although it is such a wide one today. In its place there is a modern sculpture of a monkey to commemorate its predecessor, who in the Middle Ages greeted travellers at the gate-tower before the north bank. He holds a mirror

up to onlookers, giving them a golden opportunity for a photograph with his monkey mask.

The gradient of the square clearly shows the difference in height between the bridge and the level of the foremost houses. The "Briggebuggel" has always, since time immemorial, been encircled by inns and taverns, which greeted travellers coming in from the north. They include "Alte Mühle", "Alte Brücke", "Goldener Hecht" (with a magnificent crown over the door, dating from 1717), the wide-spreading "Holländer Hof" and the "Vier Jahreszeiten" Hotel, which has a fine Madonna of its own in a corner niche. The Haspelgasse starts alongside the colourful Baroque hotel façade.

Near the middle of this wide alley the eye is taken by the striking gateway of the **Palais Cajeth** ㉕, flanked by two magnificent figures

View across the Neckar near the Old Bridge. On the left of the Brückentor ("Bridge gate") is the former Neckar school with the Tränktor, and beyond that the tower of the Jesuits' church.

The "Heidelberg Monkey" holds a mirror up to people who come to visit him.

of Hermes and the date, 1735. The building that had previously stood on this site was a medieval merchant's house with a large central hall; because of the activity here it was mentioned in 1424 as the "Tanzhaus" ("dance-hall"). The youthful Prince Elector Friedrich V gave a banquet here with 150 tables when he ceremonially entered Heidelberg with his English consort. In the Merian engraving, the house is marked as number 18 and can be recognised by its enormous saddle roof.

The historic student tavern, "Café Knösel", also represents one of the typical Heidelberg Old Town buildings which make an imposing impression by their plain and simple harmony. Here we turn off into the Untere Strasse, which also houses some Old Town taverns. The Tanzhaus already mentioned used to stretch all the way to the first crossways street, Pfaffengasse. Here we find the birthplace of the first President of the Weimar Republic, which has now been turned into the **Friedrich Ebert Memorial ㉖**. As well as looking at the cramped little

A typical alley in the Old Town: Untere Strasse. ➜

The Friedrich Ebert memorial – his birthplace. Entrance is free.

rooms, the visitor can also peruse at leisure letters and drawings, contemporary photographs, and newspaper articles about this famous Social-Democrat.

The next crossways street, Dreikönigstrasse, used to be called Judengasse ("Jews' Alley"). Although at the height of the Middle Ages Jews were not forced into a ghetto, they did live close to one another. After Ruprecht I had brought them into the town and permitted them to carry on business and even acquire property - for a fee, in the form of protection-money and taxes - his successor, Ruprecht II, simply threw them out of the town and out of his lands, impounded their property, and transferred it to the University. As a sop to conscience, their synagogue was converted to a chapel of Our Lady. A fine gateway enriches the plain façades in the Dreikönigstrasse.

Here in the lower part of the town, which used to be constantly threatened by flooding, there were not so many noble citizens' houses. One, however, the **Palais Rischer ㉗**, stands facing the entrance to Bussemergasse. The very strikingly designed main entrance, with its powerful pilasters and attractive Corinthian capitals, is in the Untere Strasse. The most remarkable feature is the deeply profiled window facings, with keystones in the form of men's heads. This fine patrician house, modelled on an Italian "Palazzo", was built in 1711 for the master-builder Rischer, who was a major force in the reconstruction of the town.

In this part of the Old Town, the other plots of land are particularly tiny, averaging only 144 square metres, so it is no wonder that the blocks are not livened up by either private or public gardens. The inhabitants do what they can with little roof-gardens, or else they move out to the pleasant suburbs; 60% of the mini-apartments here are inhabited by students. There are hardly any children to be found living in this

Aerial view of Heidelberg. A clear feature is the cramped space in the Old Town proper, above the Marstall area, distinguishing it from the more open plan of the Foregate.

district, which is not made surprising considering the innumerable inns and restaurants and the people who visit them. One black-and-white house has been nicely restored, as has house No. 16, in which Mrs Hebbel lived in 1836. At the corner of Kleine Mantelgasse, Untere Strasse opens out into the Heumarkt ("Hay Market"), enlivened by the attractive oriole of the Café Scheu. On the right is the **Sibleyhaus** ㉘, previously a hotel, "Zum Schwarzen Löwen", which once brewed its own beer.

The houses on the western side of the Grosse Mantelgasse used to stand along the old town walls, which gave the Mantelgasse its name (Mantel = cloak or covering), before Ruprecht II doubled the size of the town by extending it westwards. From the rubble of the old Mantelturm, the town walls, and the lower castle, the town had the mighty **Heuscheuer** ("Hay barn") ㉙ built as a tithe barn. Here it stored taxes paid in kind, which a the same time represented food reserves for the population. Not far from here, eastwards along the bank of the Neckar, was the town mill, also called Pfistermühle, where the store of grain was turned into flour. Although building still has a medieval look, it today houses modern lecture theatres. A plaque in the small garden opposite commemorates the synagogue which the Jewish community built here in 1877/78. It was burnt down in 1938, a victim of the Nazi reign of terror. The open square facing the Neckar is also named after the synagogue.

The **Altes Zeughaus** ("Old Arsenal") **30** adjoins the square to the south-west; it is usually called the Marstall ("Horse-stable"). The frontage on the Neckar side is 135 metres long, and used to mark the water's edge. Walls two metres thick made the single-storey building into a bulwark on the north-west corner of the town fortifications. On the courtyard side, where the walls are thinner, buttresses absorb the pressure from the vaulted roof. Where once war-material was stored for the defence of the town, nowadays students take their meals under the round towers on the north corners with their pointed turrets. Further protection, this time against the danger of fire, was supposed to be provided by the representation of a salamander (with a bearded man's head) mounted above the western entrance gate. The actual Marstall building had been put up under Prince Elector Johann Casimir on the south side of the complex, where today a modern college building stands. On the ground floor of the richly panelled, 150 metre long Renaissance building were the original stables, and on the upper floor was living accommodation. The massive roof was punctuated by five three-storey mansard windows, resulting in a building of enormous proportions. It was, however, destroyed with the town in 1693.

Hauptstrasse at the junction with Theaterstrasse. The oriole window belongs to the building which replaced the former Wormser Hof.

The foregate

The Krahnenplatz ("Crane square") adjoins the arsenal to the west. At the point where, in Merian's etching of 1620, a loading crane can be seen, the town has had a rosette worked into the pattern of the cobble-stones. A monument dating from 1897 commemorates the local poet, Karl G. Nadler.

Between Krahnenplatz and the arsenal, the romantic Schiffgasse takes us through to the Hauptstrasse. On the right is a striking Baroque building dating from 1752, the **Haus Raquet ㉛**. At the end of this alley, the eye is caught by a corner oriole in rather too bright a collection of colours, and by a gateway, both of which belong to Heidelberg's Cinema Centre. Before its destruction, this was the site of the **Wormser Hof ㉜**, which until 1610 was the town residence of the Bishops of Worms. They sold the property to Prince Elector Friedrich IV. The present-day Baroque house was built after the destruction from the remains of the old building.

If we now follow the Hauptstrasse westwards a few metres we arrive at the **Kurpfälzisches Museum ㉝** in the Palais Morass. We can see from the design of this Baroque building of 1712 that a professor at

Elegant wrought-ironwork in the inner courtyard of the Palais Morass

Kurpfälzisches Museum, Hauptstrasse 97, tel.: 583400.
More detailed information from the Museum Ticket office, openin,
hours: Tuesdays to Sundays, 10.00 a.m. to 5.00 p.m., Wednesday
until 9.00 p.m., closed on Mondays.

Tilman Riemenschneider (1460-1531): Windsheimer Altar of the Twelve Apostles, 1509.

◄ Lar the Dancer from St. Leon Rot, end of 1st century BC.

Hunting group by K.G. Lück, Frankenthal Porcelain Manufactory, about 1762. ►

Ernst Fries (1801-1833): Stift Neuburg and the Neckar Valley, 1833.

the University, Philipp Morass, was in a far better financial position than most of the citizens of Heidelberg in those desperate days. The professor built a magnificent palace on the site of the former hostel for the poor of the town, a palace which was hardly to suffer any changes during the course of the centuries. The modestly designed façade on the street side is only physically divided by round-arched gateways flanked by columns and the balcony they support. The gateway leads into a captivating courtyard which opens out into an idyllic, park-like garden. The building has belonged to the City of Heidelberg since 1905. It uses it to house the Palatinate Museum which Graimberg originally helped to found. Etchings and paintings from many centuries show the town and the castle of Heidelberg and its Princes Elector. Older by far are the two complete Frankish graves (about 600 AD), the Roman stone tablets (about 100 AD), or even the impression of the lower jaw of homo heidelbergensis (approx. 500,000 BC). Of particular artistic value is the Windsheim Altar of the Twelve Apostles, a master work by the carver Tilman Riemenschneider dating from 1509. In addition to the exhibits, the visitor will derive great pleasure from the artistic stucco ceilings and the elegant staircase, which date from the time of the reconstruction, and the magnificent banqueting room, built in 1778. It was here in the first floor that Goethe sat at table with his Prince, Karl August of Weimar, on 29th September 1815, as guests of Baroness von Zyllenhardt, the owner at the time.

Not far from the museum, on the left-hand side, the **Providenz-kirche** ㉞ comes into view. It was originally built in 1660, but had to be rebuilt again, starting in 1700. It stands on the site of the former Prince Electors' gardens, and takes its name from a saying used by Karl Ludwig (Prince Elector 1649-1680): "Dominus providebit" (The Lord shall provide). The street adjoining on the west side is also named after him.

The next street on the right, Bienenstrasse, leads us down once again to the river bank. It ends in an area dominated by the **Kongresshaus Stadthalle Heidelberg** ㉟, the congress centre. The building dates from about 1900, and is decorated all round with the heads of prominent people and ordinary citizens, and with coats-of-arms and symbols. In 1979/80, the City had its congress hall extensively and authentically restored, and equipped it at the same time with the latest technology as befits a modern congress centre. The City maintains public parks on both the narrow sides, and on the east side the Montpellierplatz, named after the French city with which Heidelberg is "twinned". On the east side the Jubiläumsplatz where in 1886 the former Zimmerplatz was replaced by a temporary festival hall on the occasion of the 500th jubilee of the University. Behind the square, between the brightly coloured façades, is a pleasing, narrow, black-and-white house which was built in the gap where formerly the Bäckergasse opened out. A few houses further

View on the town hall and the castle.

on, a tavern sign shows the original Heidelberg "Binsebub" ("sedge-boy"), a boy who once used to sell sedges for use as pipe-cleaners. The next side-street, Ziegelgasse, runs in a long and unusually flat curve to the right along the contour. It shows us today the former course of the road which led from the ford in the Neckar and gave the horse-drawn wagons a chance to take a run at the steep climb into the higher part of the foregate. It takes its name from the tileworks which stood at the end of the alley as long ago as 1363. We turn off to the left into the neighbouring Brunnengasse, and encounter the former Dominican monastery. When the principality of Palatinate came to an end, the monastery was also secularised. Prince Elector Karl Friedrich of Baden handed it over to the University and proclaimed that the cloister church should be used as a building for the **Anatomie ㊱**. The church was divided horizontally and vertically. On the ground floor the professors held their anatomy lectures in the former choir, and the nave housed the section room, preparation room, laboratory, and morgue. After 1847 the State had the present-day building built in the style of romantic classicism. The anatomy department departed for the new site on the Neuenheimer Feld in 1974.

Parallel to the Alte Anatomie in the Hauptstrasse is the three-winged **Friedrichsbau ㊲**, for which in 1860 the rest of the monastery building together with the church had to make way for this building in order to provide space for the expanding Natural Sciences faculty. The Institute of Psychology occupies the two buildings today. The monument in the Court of Honour is dedicated to the chemist

The famous chemist Robert Bunsen looks out from his low plinth towards the "Zum Riesen" house, one of the oldest citizens' houses in the town.

Bunsen, who lived and taught in Heidelberg for 44 years. The plaque on the wall of the house opposite also commemorates him; this is the **Haus zum Riesen** ("Giant house") ❸ in which Kirchhoff in 1859 applied spectral analysis, which he and Bunsen had founded, to the sun and the stars, thus opening up the chemistry of outer space. Later, the significant geologist Wilhelm Salomon-Calvi also worked here. The building had been built in 1707 in the style of the times by the Baroque master-builder Breunig for the von Venningen family, with a round-arched gateway and a balcony with a stone balustrade projecting over it. A bouquet of blossoms and fruits rises above the larger than life-size statue of the builder who gave his name to the house. Von Venningen had be given express permission by the Prince Elector's officials to use stones from the ruins of the Dicker Turm to build his house with.

We can now wander a little way westwards through Heidelberg's pedestrian precinct, which with a length of 1.6 kilometres is one of the most extensive in Germany. It is here in particular, in the central and forward part, that the department stores and smaller shops predominate. The Neugasse leads us to the left into the parallel street, called Plöck, where we are directly confronted by the **Sankt Anna Kirche 39**. It used to be part of the hospice which after 1714 took in the poor and the sick of all Christian confessions. The harmonious false cupola of the church façade was built by Rabaliatti towards the end of the 18th century. Today a modern old people's home is housed in the restored hospice.

We will now remain in Plöck to the end of our walk through the Old Town, and follow this street in the direction of Universitätsplatz. It was in Plöck in particular that the inhabitants of the former village of

Narrow Hauptstrasse leads here into the Bismarckplatz, Heidelberg's centre and a hub for all local transport.

Bergheim settled after being forced to evacuate it at the end of the 14th century. We encounter a further historic building at the very next intersection, the **Altes Waisenhaus** ("Old Orphanage") **⓾**. Originally the private Baroque home of a wealthy citizen, it served from 1756 onwards as a hospice for adherents to the reformed faith. Here Plöck opens out onto Friedrich Ebert Platz, formerly Wredeplatz, although it is separated from it by an unusual pillared structure, erected in 1927. Facing it is the sprawling building of the former **Institute of Natural Sciences ⓸**. The pavilion on the corner of the street is where Bunsen lived. At the next crossways street, Märzgasse, a small garden, the "Märzgarten", invites the passer-by to rest a while. From Märzgasse, the windows of the beautifully restored **Palais von Wieser ⓸** look out over this garden; the building dates for the early 18th century, and this is where the major legal expert von Vangerow lived from 1840 to 1870. Next door (No. 16) was where the well-known astronomer Max Wolf (1863-1932) made his name by developing the photographic method of observing stars. The founder of the Heidelberg Observatory, he had a tower-like observatory built in his parents' back yard while he was still a student, and this exists to this day.

Magnificent front face of the University library.

In Plöck No. 44 is another church, the **Erlöserkirche** (Church of the Redeemer) ❹❸. It was built in 1724 by the Dominicans, and is still used for services by Old Catholics and Anglicans, with a service in English twice a month.

Plöck opens up in a trumpet-shape at the entrance to Sandgasse between the **Peterskirche** and the **University Library** ❹❹. This was built in 1903 on the site of the Augustinian monastery. No parts have been preserved either of the typical Baroque monastery buildings or of the cloister garden, on the Plöck side, with the one exception of the gateway, which is to be seen in the museum. The library is in possession of no less than 890 manuscripts, most of them in German, returned by the Vatican from the huge "bibliotheca palatina" which was carried off in the Thirty Years War. It at least possesses copies of the other manuscripts still in Rome. The Manessiche Liederhandschrift, which belonged to Prince Elector Friedrich IV, was re-acquired in 1888 and is today the most costly witness of the book culture of the High Middle Ages.

Where the present-day Peterskirche Z stands, outside the old walls, there was in the Middle Ages a modest chapel which nonetheless served as the parish church for the town. Its place was taken in 1400

University library: Illustration of the famous pre-medieval Minnesänger (courtly poet) Walter von der Vogelweide in a very old manuscript, the Manessische Liederhandschrift.

A view through the neo-Gothic central nave of St. Peter's church, which for centuries served as the University church and mausoleum for professors.

by the Heiliggeistkirche, and King Ruprecht I gave the Peterskirche to the University. It took on its present form in 1490, but without pillars and with a flat wooden roof. A number of phases of rebuilding changed that. Today it is only the numerous gravestones of leading citizens and professors from the 15th to the 19th centuries that bear witness to the church's historical legacy.

The University Library and the Peterskirche are bordered by the Grabengasse, along which we return to the Universitätsplatz, the start of our walk through the Old Town.

Philosophenweg

From the Bismarckplatz, the Theodor Heuss bridge leads across to the north bank of the Neckar. The second cross-roads heading away from the bridge leads, if one turns right, to the beginning of Heidelberg's famous famous attraction, the Philosophenweg ("Philosophers' Road"). It first climbs very steeply up-hill. At the only side-turning we encounter various buildings belonging to institutes in the Faculty of Physics and Astronomy. The road now levels out and offers unique views across the river, the city, the castle, and the wooded Königstuhl hills (568 metres above sea level). When we get to the carefully tended Philosophengärtchen we are at the same height as the ruins of the castle. Here hikers will find two stone signposts, such as are to be found all over the Heidelberg Stadtwald ("municipal forest"). The steep path above the park leads to the Eichendorff park, where a memorial plaque commemorates the romantic poet who studied in Heidelberg in 1807/08. Above this is the Oberer Philosophenweg, which must be the point from which Merian created his etching of Heidelberg in 1620.

A wider view, however, is provided by the lower Philosophenweg, which leads us along the side of the Heiligenberg hill. Two small gardens are dedicated to Liselotte von der Pfalz and to the poet Hölderlin, together with his romantic ode to Heidelberg, "Lange lieb' ich dich schon ... "

Next to the Hölderlin garden is the start of a road which leads us via the Hirschgasse down into the valley. Before we reach the Ziegelhaüser Landstrasse at the bottom we pass a group of buildings, the Hotel Hirschgasse, formerly the students' "Paukboden" - a place where duels were fought with live ammunition. Here innumerable fencing duels were fought (purely as sport) while duels to the death were fought in the adjoining woods.

It was in the Ziegelhaüser Landstrasse, on this section between the Schleusensteg (the path across the locks) and the Alte Brücke, that Viktor von Scheffel lived as a law student. It is to him that we owe one of the world-famous songs about this city on the Neckar: "Alt' Heidelberg, du feine, du Stadt an Ehren reich" ("Old Heidelberg, you fine city, you city rich in honours").

Philosophenweg:
A memorial to Liselotte von der Pfalz, the unhappy daughter of a Prince Elector.

Handschuhsheim

Leaving the Theodor Heuss bridge one passes through the suburb of Neuenheim, where once the Roman settlement stood, and a kilometre further this merges almost unnoticed into the suburb of Handschuhsheim. Where the main road bears away to the left, the Steubenstrasse leads straight ahead into the centre of the old village (first mentioned in documents in AD 765). The Steubenstrasse ends at the "Tiefburg", a moated castle dating from the 13th century which, like Heidelberg and the whole region, fell victim to the War of Succession in 1689/93. There is a charming Schlösschen ("little castle") at Tiefburgplatz, with an elegant stair tower and Baroque "onion dome". This former country mansion is now the home of the municipal School of Music and Song.

From the adjoining park one can at once make out the walls of Heidelberg's oldest church, St Vitus. The forbidding west tower is all that is left of the 11th century building. The nave and the choir were altered into the Gothic style in 1483, and the modern part added at the side in 1933. The parts worth seeing are the 15th century frescoes and the significant double tombs in the former choir of the church, with the brother and sister Hans and Barbara on the left and their parents opposite, Heinrich von Handschuhsheim and Amale Beusser of Ingelheim. The inscriptions narrate the tragic fate of the family, particularly the mother, who lost her husband in 1588, her daughter in 1599, and her 15-year-old son a year later, at which point the family died out. Hans met his death

Ruins of St. Michael Basilica on the Heiligenberg. ➤

St. Vitus church: Memorial to the family of Heinrich von Handschuhsheim.

in a duel with the equally youthful Friedrich von Hirschhorn on the market place in Heidelberg. Both tombs were masterfully created in the style of the Renaissance, and the items of clothing are so diligently crafted that one could be looking at the latest fashions. The two other double tombs commemorate "Dyther" von Handschuhsheim (who died in 1487) and Margaretha von Handschuhsheim (1500). Both tombs are designed in the late Gothic style, with the latter with its fully detailed figures being the most artistic one in the St Vitus church.

Heiligenberg

From Tiefburgplatz one can easily travel by car to the top of the Heiligenberg, where there is a car-park. Nearby we can still discern the foundation walls of the Stephankloster and its little chapel, built in the 11th century by the monks from the neighbouring Michaelkloster. Both were abandoned about 1500, and fell into ruin.

Members of a local conservation association built an observation tower in 1885 from the remains of the Stephankloster, in a highly romantic style. The view is breath-taking from here: from a height of 375 metres above sea level one can see over to the deep notch of the Neckar valley, the roofs of the Old Town, and downwards onto the ruined castle in front of the massive Königstuhl hills.

There are another 65 metres to climb to the main peak. The Nazis had a "germanische Thingstätte" built between the various peaks in

1935, using forced labour from the Arbeitsdienst; this was planned to be a kind of open-air ceremonial theatre. By climbing its steps, or walking up the forest path next to it, we come to the highest point of the hill. Memorial plaques tell of the Celts, who lived in this area between 500 and 100 BC. Up here they built a fort of refuge for protection against the German tribes moving into their area. It consisted of two ring-shaped mounds, the outer one 3 kilometres and the inner one of 2 kilometres in circumference, each with two entrances cut through them. Inside these mounds was a settlement with pasture for the cattle between the two rings. The Michaelkloster stood right at the summit of the hill. It was founded in 870 by monks from Lorsch. At the turn of the millennium they built the Basilica in the Roman style and dedicated it to "All Saints". This is how the Heiligenberg (literally: Saints' Hill) came by its name. The foundation walls which have been dug out show today how impressive the buildings of the old monastery were. Like the Stephankloster, it was abandoned in about 1500.

Neuenheim

Although this part of the city was the centre of the settlement in the Heidelberg area during Roman times, until the beginning of the 20th century it merely played the role of a dormitory suburb surrounded by gardens and open fields. The University administration had begun making plans back in 1912 for removing the natural sciences faculties out to the Neuenheimer Feld, but it was not until 1936 that the Surgical Clinic was ceremonially opened as the first complex of buildings west of the Berliner Strasse. It was then followed by one new building after another on this site, which is now larger in extent than the Old Town. Next to it came the gigantic complex of the German Cancer Research Centre (1972). The old Botanical Garden is now completely surrounded by university buildings, whilst the very remarkable zoo, the sports facilities, the youth hostel, and the city open-air swimming pool are pushed in like a defence wall between the developed area and the Neckar. Behind the University sports facilities, room has been found for the German National Competitive Sports Centre for swimming, basket-ball, volley-ball, and table tennis.

Königstuhl ("King's Throne")

This is the second highest hill in the Odenwald range, 568 metres high; the only higher one is the Katzenbuckel near Eberbach. Anyone who lives in Heidelberg has several possible ways of clambering up the hill in his back garden: the easy, winding way on foot, with rather more sweat straight up the "Himmelsleiter" ("Ladder to Heaven"), by car starting from the Friedrich Ebert Anlage or the Rohrbacher

Old mountain railway at the top of the Königstuhl.

← *New mountain railway between the town walls and Molkenkur.*

Strasse, or, the really decent way, with the cable railway. The lower part of this railway, which has now been modernised, has since 1890 led from Kornmarkt to the intermediate station "Schloss" and on up to "Molkenkur". This is where Heidelberg's second castle used to stand, until it was struck by lightning in 1537. This was the point from which Tilly besieged the castle and the town in 1623, until both were conquered, for the first time in history. The hill takes its name from the Molkenkuranstalt which operated here from the middle of the 19th century onwards. Its owner kept anything up to 50 goats from the milk of which he produced cheese and a new product, milk curds, regarded in those days as a cure for anaemia. The present-day hill-top restaurant conceals the core of this building within its walls, and also provides a magnificent view out across the Odenwald and the Rhine plain.

In 1907 the mountain railway struggled up the 280 metres with considerable rumblings, but reliably and in a straight line. At the top, a magnificent view from the terraces of the upper station and the hill-top restaurant awaits the visitor, and if visibility is particularly good it is worth while going on up to the observation tower. Numerous paths allow exploration of the very flat, heavily wooded top of the hill, and concealed in them is a "children's-stories paradise" and the astronomical observatory (1898). The Max Planck Institute for Astronomy was built in the vicinity in 1976.

The Königstuhl falls away gradually to the south and is accessible by a close-knit network of paths. The instructions and arrows on the big stones at each cross-roads lead the hiker to many places well worth seeing: the Kohlhof with its steep orchards, which provide Heidlebergers with ski-ing in the winter, the specialist hospital and the Posseltsluststurm tower, the Drei Eichen cross-roads, and the Blockhaus with a magnificent group of rhododendrons planted in 1904 and the mammoth trees of 100 years old.

On the western slopes of this wooded area, near the Speyerhof hospital and the city's own operating farm, the Bierhelder Hof, there is a military cemetery first laid out in 1934 which impressively symbolises the "Road to Eternity". The name of 520 soldiers who were killed in battle or died of wounds are chiselled into the 28 gigantic blocks of stone, each weighing 130 hundredweight, which mark the edges of the central road. After the second world war a second graveyard was laid out to the left of the "march of advance" road with a temple of honour dedicated to the young men whose lives were even more senselessly sacrificed.

The main axis of the military cemetery points exactly at the graveyard in front of the western part of the modern city of Heidelberg. Here a large number of leading personalities have found their last rest: the first President of the German Republic after the departure of the Kaiser, Friedrich Ebert, the conductor Wilhelm Furtwängler, the conservator of the castle Count Graimberg, the chemist Robert Bunsen, the local poet Nadler, and many others. Heidelberg was, in 1891, one of the first cities to build a crematorium for its central graveyard, thus making cremation possible.

An excursion along the Neckar valley

The passenger ships of the "White Fleet" anchor opposite the Congress Centre. Travelling up-stream along the famous Neckar valley we soon leave the tightly packed buildings in the heart of the city behind us. The hills close in on either side of the river, and along the bank there is in places only room for roads and the railway line. Where the valley opens out to the left into sloping meadows, we can see a group of buildings on the bank which form the Hotel Haarlass. This is where one of the two tile-works of the neighbouring convent, Neuburg, used to stand, which greets us brightly and merrily from the hill above. Parts of the building dating from about 1300 are still preserved in the heart of the present-day cloister church. During the course of the centuries the buildings served monks and nuns (from 1195 onwards) as a home and a place for divine services, until the cloister was dissolved in 1562 and converted into a convent for unmarried ladies from noble families. A major Goethe memorial was set up here in the 19th century, and the building has belonged to the Benedictine Order again since 1929. In addition to exemplary agricultural and horticultural work, the monks are well know for breeding ivy.

The tile-works (Ziegeleien) of the former cloister provided the name for the part of the town behind the Neuburg convent, Ziegelhausen. A bridge links it with the small town of Schlierbach on the opposite bank. After travelling through one more set of locks and on for another 6 kilometres or so, we reach the old Free Imperial City of Neckargemünd, which has a picturesque centre. It was from here that Tilly, in 1622, tried in vain to storm the nearby castle of Dilsberg, the only one in the region to stand up to his troops. Visible from far away, it rises on a hill rounded by the Neckar, its turrets proudly uplifted to the sky. From up there one can enjoy a magnificent panorama of the curves of the Neckar and to Neckarsteinach, the "Town of the Four Castles". The lords of these castles had the title of "Landschaden" ("despoiler of the countryside") of Steinach, having inherited this dubious honour from their ancestor, a landless brigand called Bligger von Steinach. The tombs of this noble family can be seen in the Evangelical church in Neckarsteinach, which is where the river excursion from Heidelberg usually ends.

Neckargemünd, once a Free Imperial City, with its carefully manicured frontage on the Neckar between the parish churches.

91

Special events

The Heidelberg event that attracts most visitors is without any doubt the floodlighting of the castle which takes place, in conjunction with a grand firework display from the Alte Brücke, about three times each summer. The best view is to be had from the right bank of the Neckar, from Philosophenweg, and from the Theodor Heuss bridge, although it is not possible here to avoid a very dense crowd. The famous castle flood-lighting is a reminder of the great fires of 1689/93 and 1764, when the Residence of the Princes Elector went up in flames. On 20th July 1807, huge log fires were lit in the

Schlossgarten in honour of Prinz Karl of Baden and his consort. This was the first castle illuminations, the next followed in 1815 and 1830, once again to honour noble guests. In 1860 the castle ruins were illuminated with "Bengal fire", as is done to tremendous effect today.

In the summer months there are also theatrical performances in the castle, against the backdrop of the magnificent buildings built by Ottheinrich and Friedrich IV. The most famous is the English version of the romantic musical "The Student Prince", which has also been filmed. Both events contribute to spreading the wonder of Heidelberg all over the world.

Illuminations of the Castle and the bridges in Heidelberg with a brilliant firework display above the Old Town.

Winter's atmosphere in Heidelberg

The Palace and Palace Garden Schwetzingen

Only 12 km to the West of Heidelberg lies the former summer residence of the Elector of the Palatinate, the imposing Palace of Schwetzingen.

At the beginning of the 18th century the old water castle was transformed into the electoral summer palace as it is in its present form. From 1750 onwards, when the interior of the palace became too restrictive for the baroque style of the Court, the Elector, Carl Theodor of the Palatinate, had two representative rooms constructed in two quarter-circle circular houses. The resultant semi-circle formed the basis for the construction of the 72 ha large Schwetzingen Palace Gardens, which were, and still are, among the most important artistic and cultural gardens in Europe.

Magnificent show of tulips in the Schwetzingen Palace Gardens.

The special feature of the Schwetzingen Palace Gardens is the close proximity of a strictly French-style baroque form garden, created by the Architects Johann Ludwig Petri and Nicolas de Pigage, and a so-called English Country Garden, which was the work of Friedrich Ludwig Sckell (later the designer of the English Garden "Englischer Garten" in Munich) and then of Johann Michael Zeyher. Whilst most of the baroque gardens became victims of the Enlightenment, so popular at the time, the Schwetzingen Gardens were left unaltered and aptly surrounded by a Country Garden, so that both can be admired at the same time. Since 1970 the Palace Garden has seen successive reconstruction according to historic plans and now reflects again a great deal of authenticity.

Bergbahnen Heidelberg

HSB

"One is conveyed from the hustle and bustle of the town to the perfect peace and tranquillity of the forest in such a short space of time." (1890)

Allow Heidelberg to enchant you and take a ride on the over 100 year old funicular railway to the castle, *Königstuhl* and Fairy Tale Paradise. Enjoy the view of the town and countryside. The bus lines 11 and 33 take you to the downhill station at the *Kornmarkt*, bus stop *Rathaus/Bergbahn*.

The Ride

From the *Kornmarkt* station, our ground funicular pulls you up
to the castle, the *Molkenkur* and then up to the *Königstuhl*. You
can change at the *Molkenkur* and take the second train, which sti
has wooden carriages and which dates back to 1907. You can als
break the trip at whichever station you like.

The Technology

To begin with, the funicular railway system consisted of a headwhee
at the *Molkenkur* station around which a steel cable ran; a coacl
was attached to each end of this cable.

Water tanks with a volume of 8 cubic metres were built into th
coaches and to operate the system, the tank in the top coach wa
filled with water until it started to move downhill as a result of
the excess weight, thereby pulling the coach attached to the oth
end uphill.

The upper line to the *Königstuhl* overcomes a height of 261 metre
The upper railway travels at a speed of 2 m/sec, the lower one a
3 m/sec.

Thanks to a nicely fitted visitors' room, it is now possible to hav
a look at the machinery that operates the *Königstuhl* railway syster

The Special Offer

Using the HSB package deal, four persons can travel with the funicular railway in the period between Good Friday and All Saints' Day. In addition to this, you have the option of using the tower elevator to enjoy the pleasures of the Fairy Tale Paradise.

Additional Information

is available from the Mobility Consultancy mobil 2001 at the *Bismarckplatz*, which is open from Monday to Friday, 9.30 am to 12.30 pm and 1.15 to 5.15 pm.

or ask for our free brochure:
Tel: 0 62 21 / 5 13-26 09

http://www.hvv-heidelberg.de

How to get to the funicular railway

HSB
Heidelberger Straßen- und Bergbahn Aktiengesellschaft

The *Bismarckplatz* is Heidelberg's main traffic junction. Our buses and trains travel in all directions from there.

Your way to our funicular railway from the *Bismarckplatz*

▨▨▨ on foot

▨ by bus

▮ by car

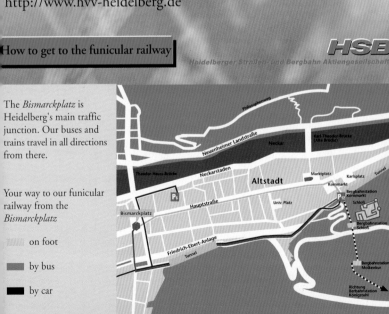

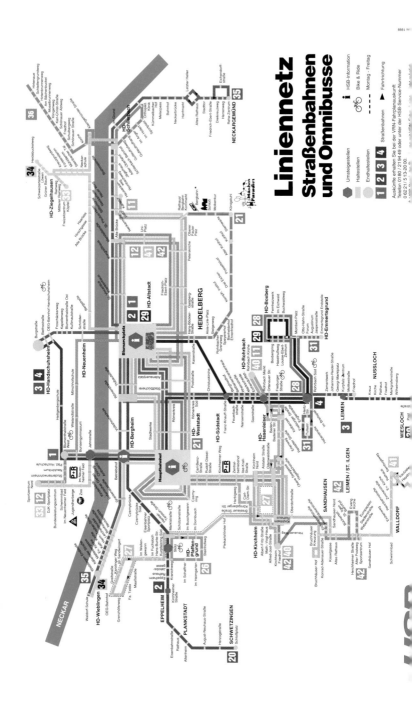

Liniennetz
Straßenbahnen und Omnibusse

i HSB-Information

🚲 Bike & Ride

– – – – Montag - Freitag

▲ Fahrtrichtung

⬡ Umsteigestellen

○ Haltestellen

● Endhaltestellen

1 2 3 4 Straßenbahnen

Auskünfte erhalten Sie bei der VRN-Fahrplanauskunft
Telefon 01 80 / 2 19 44 49 oder unter der HSB-Service-Nummer
0 62 21 / 5 13-20 00.

The deer fountain in the Schwetzingen castle garden.

Nicolas de Pigage designed some splendid architectural creations for the garden, such as the bath house with the large oval basin made from white marble, the fantastically graceful mosque or the Apollo temple.

His greatest achievement however was the magnificent Rococo Theatre, the shell of which he constructed in 1752 within the unbelievably short time of only 10 weeks. Today the theatre has a technically modern stage, whilst the actual construction of the auditorium remains to a great extent in its original form. The Rococo Theatre is annually the site for the internationally recognized Schwetzinger Festspiele (Schwetzingen Festival) and many other theatre presentations and concerts and, during the summer months, it can be viewed four times daily during stage demonstrations.

The Palace building itself was extensively renovated up to 1991 and historic records were consulted to ensure that it was provided with original fittings of the 18th and 19th century. Apart from the magnificent rooms of the Electoral Couple, visitors to the Palace can also admire the living standard of the Court during the baroque period.

Guided tours of the Palace are available daily except Mondays.

The Palace Garden is open daily to visitors throughout the year.

Practical tips from A to Z:

Accommodation Office: Tourist information at the main railway station, Tel. 2 77 35/2 13 41

Ambulance: Tel. 85888

Apothekenmuseum (Apothecary's Museum): In the Ottheinrichsbau in the Castle, Tel. 16 57 80. Open daily 10 a.m. to 5.30 p.m.

Archaeological Institute: Marstallhof, open Wednesdays from 15.00 to 19.00 h., Sun 11.00 to 13.00 h., Tel. 54 25 12

Art Club: Hauptstr. 97, Tel. 18 40 86, Varying exhibitions

Bicycle rental:
PerBike,
Bergheimer Strasse 125, Tel. 16 11 08

Boat hire: Theodor-Heuss-Brücke (bridge) and Congress building, Tel. 41 19 25

Botanical Garden: Im Neuenheimer Feld 340, Tel. 54 57 38, open Mondays to Thursdays, Sundays and Public Holidays 09.00 to 12.00 and 13.00 to 16.00 hours, closed Fridays and Saturdays

Bundesbahn (Federal Railways) Information: Tel. 1 94 19

Camping sites: HD-Schlierbach, Tel. 80 25 06, Haide (between Ziegelhausen and Neckargemünd), Tel. 06 2 23/21 11

Car rental: Avis, Tel. 2 22 15; Hertz, Tel. 2 34 34 Europ Car, Tel. 5 39 90

Castle: Enquiries at the Castle Booking Office, Tel. 53 84 14 or Castle Management, Tel. 53840, Fax 16 77 02

Castle festivals: (Open air performances in the Heidelberg Castle) End of July to End of August, Tel. 58 35 21, 12760

Castle illumination: 3 times during the year
1st Saturday in June
2nd Saturday in July
1st Saturday in September

Cinemas: Lux-Harmonie, Tel. 2 20 00; Kammer, Tel. 2 15 50; Kamera, Tel. 40 98 02; Studio-Europa, Tel. 2 56 00; Schloß, Tel. 2 05 25; Gloria, Tel. 2 53 19

Customs and Excise Office: Kurfürstenanlage 25, Tel. 5 30 60

Emergency – Police: Tel. 1 10

Events: Concerts, cabaret, sport, theatre and exhibitions – full information from Verkehrsverein Heidelberg (Tourist Information Office), Tel. 1 94 33

Event organisations:
Heidelberg Incoming Touristik (HIT) Heidelberg, Obere Neckarstraße 31–33 Tel. 06 2 21/2 96 41 and 1 27 60, Fax 18 49 17 and Congress & Incoming Service Heidelberg GmbH, Alte Bergheimer Straße 6, Tel. 06 2 21/ 16 60 97–99, Fax 12 11 12 + 18 10 19

Excursion by ship: Rhein-Neckar Fahrgastschiffahrt, Tel. 2 01 81. Personenschiffahrt Hornung, Tel. 48 00 64

Fire: Tel. 1 12

Guided Tours: Congress & Incoming Service Heidelberg GmbH, Alte Bergheimer Strasse 6, 69115 Heidelberg, Tel. 16 60 97

Guided tours of the inside of the Castle: included in the entry price for the courtyard and Großes Faß. Opening times:
1st April–31st October, daily from 09.00–17.00 hours, 1st November–31st March, daily from 09.00–16.00 hours. Group tours on request, guide ticket offices in the Castle courtyard, Tel. 53 84 14, Fax 16 77 02

Guided tours on foot: April to October 2.00 pm every day in German/English; November to March, Saturday, in German only. Meeting point: Universitätsplatz (Lion Fountain) at 2.00 pm. Tour lasts about 2 hours. Information from Heidelberg Verkehrsverein, Tel. 1 94 33

Guided tours by bus: April to October, Thursday, 2.00 pm; Friday/Saturday, 10.00 am and 2.00 pm; November to March, Saturday, 2.00 pm; in German/ English. Sunday and public holidays: 10 pm. Advance seat reservation necessary at the Heidelberg Verkehrsverein, Tel. 1 94 33, Fax 16 73 18

Indoor swimming pools: In the "DHC", Am Bismarckplatz, Tel. 58 19 60; "Emmertsgrund", Im Bürgerhaus, Tel. 38 30 27; "Hasenleiser", Erlenweg, Tel. 31 01 51; "Köpfl", Tel. 80 06 22

Kurpfälzisches Museum (Palatinate Museum): Hauptstr. 97, Tel. 5 84 34 02, open Tuesday–Sunday 10.00–17.00 hours, Wed. to 21.00 hours, Monday closed

Lost Property Office: Bergheimer Strasse 69, Tel. 58 13 80

Märchenparadies Königstuhl (Magical Paradise Königstuhl): Königstuhl 5a, Tel. 2 34 16, open March to October, daily 10.00 to 18.00 hours, June to August, daily 10.00 to 19.00 hours

Medical emergency service: Tel. 1 92 92

Mountain Railway: Tel. 2 27 96, from Talstation (valley station) Kornmarkt to the Castle, Molkenkur and Königstuhl stations

Municipal Authority: Rathaus (Town Hall) Marktplatz 10, Tel. 5 80

Old University: Studentenkarzer (students' prison): Augustinergasse, Tel. 54 23 34. Tuesday to Friday, 10.00 am to 12.00 noon and 2.00 to 5.00 pm, also between 10.00 am and 1.00 pm on Saturdays from 1st April to 31st October. Closed on Sundays, Mondays, and public holidays.

Police: Römerstrasse 2, Tel. 9 90

Post office branches: Belfortstrasse, Sofienstrasse, Grabengasse

Reichspräsident-Friedrich-Ebert-Gedenkstätte (Federal President Friedrich Ebert Memorial) Pfaffengasse 18, Tel. 9 10 70, Guided Tours on request. Open Tuesday–Sunday 10.00–18.00 hours and Thursdays 10.00–20.00 hours

Schloßhof and Großes Faß (Palace Courtyard and Big Barrel) Open: 1st April–31st October, daily from 09.00–17.00 hours, 1st November–31st March daily from 10.00–16.00 hours. Free access to the courtyard outside the official opening times is possible as long as no special events are taking place. The Großes Faß is freely accessible up to 1 hour after the booking office has been closed

Schwetzingen Palace Events: Tel. 0 62 02/49 33

Sightseeing tour of the town: Heidelberger Straßen + Bergbahn AG (HSB), departure: near the Bismarckplatz and main railway station; May–October: daily 10.00 + 14.00 hours, November–March, only Saturdays at 14.00 hours; April: daily 14.00 hours. Tel. 2 22 21 and 5 13 27 57

Sternwarte (Observatory) Heidelberg-Königstuhl: Tel. 50 90, Guided tour on request

Studentenkarzer (Students' prison): Augustinergasse, Tel. 54 23 34: open from April–Oct., Tues.–Fri. 10 a.m. to 4 p.m. Closed on Mon., Sat., Sun. and public Holiday

Taxi: Tel. 30 20 30

Textile museum: Ziegelhausen, The Old evangelical Church, Wednesday, Saturday and Sunday, 13.00–18.00 hours, Tel. 80 03 17

Theatres: Städtische Bühne, Theaterstraße 8, Tel. 5 83 5 20/21; Zimmertheater, Hauptstraße 118, Tel. 2 10 69; In der "Alten Krone", Brückenkopfstraße 1, Tel. 4 41 49; Im Romanischen Keller, Seminarstraße, Tel. 47 16 79

Tour Guide Club: HD-Kirchheim, Gleiwitzer Str. 12, Tel. 78 17 25, – Fax: 78 62 18

Tourist information: 69115 Heidelberg: Am Hauptbahnhof, P.O. Box 10 58 60 (mainline railway station), Tel. 1 94 33. Monday to Saturday, 9.00 am to 7.00 pm; Sunday, 10.00 am to 6.00 pm. Additional information during the tourist season at Neckarmünzplatz and at the Castle station of the mountain railway

Town library: Open Tuesday–Friday 10.00–20.00 hours, Saturday 10.00–16.00 hours. Tel. 5 83 6 13/14, Poststr. 15

University Library: Exhibition room, Plöck 107–109, Tel. 54 23 80

Verkehrsverein (Tourist Office): Friedrich-Ebert-Anlage 2, Stadtgarten, Tel. 14 22 11

Völkerkunde-Museum (Museum of Ethnology): Hauptstrasse 235, Tel. 2 20 67

Youth Hostel: Tiergartenstraße 5, Tel. 41 20 66, only with valid Youth Hostel Identity Card

Zoo: Tiergartenstraße, open 09.00–19.00 hours, during Winter 09.00–17.00 hours, Tel. 48 00 41